STRONGMAN

Also by Kenneth C. Davis

In the Shadow of Liberty

More Deadly Than War

KENNETH C. DAVIS

STRONGMAN

THE RISE OF
FIVE
DICTATORS
AND THE FALL OF
DEMOCRACY

Henry Holt and Company
New York

TO KIT AND ARCHER . . .
HOPE AND LOVE

Henry Holt and Company, *Publishers since 1866*
Henry Holt® is a registered trademark of Macmillan Publishing Group, LLC
120 Broadway, New York, NY 10271 • mackids.com

Library of Congress Cataloging-in-Publication Data
Names: Davis, Kenneth C., author.
Title: Strongman : the rise of five dictators and the fall of democracy /
Kenneth C. Davis.
Description: First edition. | New York : Henry Holt & Co, 2020. | Includes
bibliographical references and index. | Audience: Ages 12–18 | Summary:
"A nonfiction account of some of the deadliest dictators in modern
history"—Provided by publisher.
Identifiers: LCCN 2020009793 | ISBN 9781250205643 (hardcover)
Subjects: LCSH: Dictators—Biography—Juvenile literature. |
Dictatorship—History—20th century—Juvenile literature. |
Democracy—History—Juvenile literature. | Hitler, Adolf,
1889-1945—Juvenile literature. | Stalin, Joseph, 1878-1953—Juvenile
literature. | Mao, Zedong, 1893-1976—Juvenile literature. | Hussein,
Saddam, 1937-2006—Juvenile literature.
Classification: LCC D412.7 .D28 2020 | DDC 321.9092/2—dc23
LC record available at https://lccn.loc.gov/2020009793
ISBN 978-1-250-20564-3

Our books may be purchased in bulk for promotional, educational, or business use. Please
contact your local bookseller or the Macmillan Corporate and Premium Sales Department
at (800) 221-7945 ext. 5442 or by email at MacmillanSpecialMarkets@macmillan.com.

First edition, 2020 / Designed by Kay Petronio
Printed in the United States of America by LSC Communications, Harrisonburg, Virginia
1 3 5 7 9 10 8 6 4 2

CONTENTS

But the principles on which the constitution of the American states rest, the principles of order, balance of powers, true liberty, and sincere and deep respect for law, are indispensable for all republics; they should be common to them all; and it is safe to forecast that where they are not found the republic will soon have ceased to exist.

—**Alexis de Tocqueville,** *Democracy in America*

Power is not a means; it is an end. One does not establish a dictatorship in order to safeguard a revolution; one makes the revolution in order to establish the dictatorship. The object of persecution is persecution. The object of torture is torture. The object of power is power.

—**George Orwell,** *1984*

INTRODUCTION

DICTATORS,

DESPOTS,

AND

DEMOCRACY

Tyranny naturally arises out of democracy.

—**Plato,** *The Republic*

• • •

We here highly resolve that these dead shall not have
died in vain—that this nation, under God, shall have a new
birth of freedom—and that government of the people, by
the people, for the people, shall not perish from the earth.

—**Abraham Lincoln,** Gettysburg Address

WHO ARE THEY?

Adolf Hitler as an infant.
[Wikimedia Commons]

One was a boy who loved to read fanciful tales of America's Old West and play at being a cowboy. With dreams of being a great artist, he only wanted to draw and paint.

Another dropped out of the seminary where he was training to be a priest and later worked briefly as a meteorologist making weather charts.

And still a third was a bullied schoolboy who balked at an arranged marriage at the age of fourteen, then registered to join a police academy and a soap-making school before working as a librarian's assistant.

Joseph Stalin in a 1902 police mug shot. [Wikimedia Commons]

Little in their early years hints that these men—Adolf Hitler, Joseph Stalin, and Mao Zedong—would become three of the most murderous dictators in history. They chafed at the plans their fathers made for them. As young men beginning to find their way in the world, they were certainly rebellious, as many teenagers and students are. Yet all became capable of ordering the deaths of tens of millions of people through war, starvation, forced labor, and

Earliest known portrait of Mao, around 1913.
[Wikimedia Commons]

mass extermination. They achieved their genocidal legacies with the consent and complicity of many loyal disciples, obedient generals, secret police forces, willing politicians, and vast numbers of the people they ruled.

How could they do it? How *did* they do it?

This book tells how a Strongman—a dictator or autocrat with unlimited control—gains that power. It shows how such a leader ruthlessly suppresses dissent and eliminates enemies, real or imagined. It is also the story of how a leader can wipe out any semblance of the freedoms that many Americans and people in other democracies may take for granted today, including free speech, the freedom to worship—or not—and the freedom of the press.

Each of the five men discussed in this book—Benito Mussolini of Italy, Germany's Adolf Hitler, Joseph Stalin of the Soviet Union, China's Mao Zedong, and Saddam Hussein of Iraq— were responsible for genocidal crimes against humanity with unthinkable numbers of victims. Stalin killed millions of people well before World War II began, in 1939. The grim death toll mounted as Hitler's Germany and the Soviet Union fought each other in that war, and then, with Mussolini's assistance, the Nazis began the "Final Solution," mass executions, starvation, and other war crimes. Mao Zedong, who secured Communist control over China in 1949, was responsible, historians now contend, for the deaths of at least forty-five million people. The leader of a tyrannical regime in Iraq for decades before he was overthrown by the United States in 2003, Saddam Hussein employed torture, chemical weapons, mass executions, and wars against neighboring countries to secure his place in the list of infamous killers.

"One death is a tragedy; a million deaths is a statistic." This quote, attributed to Stalin, reminds us that reading such astonishing numbers can be mind-numbing.

But we must never become unfeeling. This book is not a list of faceless statistics. Neither is it an encyclopedia of the worst atrocities of fascism, Nazism, Communism, and other *-isms*. It is a collection of portraits of men who caused unthinkable death and destruction. By exploring the lives of some of the twentieth century's most deadly dictators, this book sets out to put a human face on inhumanity. It looks at who these men were; how they were able to gain such unlimited power; what they shared in common; and how the people they ruled—either willingly or under a reign of terror—followed their murderous paths.

History is often a matter of emphasis. It can be presented as an eye-glazing list of dates and numbers. Or it can be told as heroic, rousing tales of "great men" to stir pride and patriotism. But sometimes history is something else. Often, it is simply horrible. This history contains an ugly catalog of crimes and injustice. It is about executions, unspeakable torture, and secret police forces coming in the night to spread terror among common citizens. It is about genocide.

Many visitors to the U.S. Holocaust Memorial Museum in Washington, D.C., are brought to tears by a display of shoes. Each victim of this mass murder was a person, and these shoes belonged to some of the millions of people who were consigned to death in the Nazi gas chambers and labor camps.

Shoes of the victims of Auschwitz.
[Wikimedia Commons]

These shoes remind us that history is about people—real, ordinary people.

Strongman, then, is a human story—the story of real people doing terrible things to other people. Telling this story is difficult because it is so dreadful and yet cannot be sugarcoated. There is no way to adequately discuss the countless deaths and horrific misery these leaders left in their wake without laying bare the specific horror of their crimes against humanity. These crimes include beatings, rapes, individual acts of murder, deliberate starvation, and mass exterminations—all grim, but unfortunately too real to explain away and too dangerous to ignore.

Telling these stories has been made even more difficult because the lives of these men have been cloaked in misconceptions and continuing propaganda. Today, pilgrims visit the burial sites of Mussolini, Stalin, and Mao Zedong, drawn by nostalgic recollections of men celebrated as great national leaders, not murderous dictators. Propaganda upends, twists, and denies fact. But facts are stubborn things. If history is really supposed to help us learn from the past, we must relentlessly look for truth to answer some important questions:

☆ **What turns a seemingly ordinary man into a monstrous killer?**

☆ **What makes a country fall prey to a dictator at the cost of millions of lives?**

☆ **Is democracy the most desirable government?**

☆ **If democracy is desirable, how do we safeguard it?**

These are crucial issues. Around the globe today, political leaders—some elected legitimately—have begun whittling away at civil liberties, human rights, religious freedom, and the established rule of law. They use suppression of the media, mass arrests, and assassinations of people considered political threats or "enemies of the people"—journalists among them. Authoritarian rulers make widespread use of propaganda, or "fake news," to manipulate public opinion. And very often, they target some group—immigrants, one particular race, or religious minorities—as scapegoats for a country's ills.

In March 2020, Freedom House, an international organization that monitors democracy around the world, issued a report that said that global freedom had declined for the fourteenth consecutive year. "Democracy and pluralism are under assault. Dictators are toiling to stamp out the last vestiges of domestic dissent and spread their harmful influence to new corners of the world. At the same time, many freely elected leaders are dramatically narrowing their concerns to a blinkered interpretation of the national interest. In fact, such leaders—including the chief executives of the United States and India, the world's two largest democracies—are increasingly willing to break down institutional safeguards and disregard the rights of critics and minorities as they pursue their populist agendas . . . The protests of 2019 have so far failed to halt the overall slide in global freedom, and without greater support and solidarity from established democracies, they are more likely to succumb to authoritarian reprisals."

For that reason, this book is also about democracy. It opens with a case study of how quickly a democracy can die. It then offers a short biography of democracy as an idea.

Democracy is a fragile flower, as the opening chapters will show. When the U.S. Constitution was being written in 1787, Founding Father Benjamin Franklin worried that the United States might end up with an elected monarch. Some two

Bust of Plato. [Wikimedia Commons]

thousand years earlier, the Greek philosopher Plato predicted that democracy—an idea born in ancient Greece—would end in tyranny.

Were they right?

The stories of the five men presented here pose even more difficult questions. Examining their repressive systems forces us to ask whether the bleak picture predicted in *1984*, George Orwell's nightmarish dystopian novel, is the way the world will go. Written in the aftermath of World War II as the Soviet Union extended its totalitarian hold over Eastern Europe, Orwell's book envisioned a world divided among three superpowers constantly at war, a bleak world in which personal freedom and individuality have vanished and many Party members wear the same blue overalls. Will Orwell's Big Brother displace Lady Liberty? Will his frightening Newspeak—a language controlled by the government—crush objective facts? Will history go down the "memory hole" in ashes, as it does in Orwell's Ministry of Truth, where records are destroyed and constantly rewritten to serve the state?

And finally, we are left with the hardest question of all. It is a personal one. "If faced with a Strongman, what would I do?"

You've probably heard the popular expression "to die for." Maybe a friend has said, "Those shoes are to die for."

Of course, we don't really mean we would give our lives willingly for a beautiful pair of shoes. But that figure of speech raises the ultimate question: What, if anything, would you be willing to die for?

Family? Friends? Faith?

The first draft of the Declaration of Independence is presented to Congress in this 1818 painting by John Trumbull. The men who signed the Declaration would pledge, "our Lives, our Fortunes, and our sacred Honor" to the cause of liberty. [Architect of the Capitol]

In 1776, the men who signed the Declaration of Independence pledged "our Lives, our Fortunes, and our sacred Honor" to the cause of freedom. Those words were more than flowery sentiments. They reflected the enormous risk taken by those fifty-six men in the cause of some timeless ideas: that "all men are created equal," that we are entitled to "Life, Liberty and the pursuit of Happiness," and that governments can only obtain "their just powers from the consent of the governed." The idea that we consent in the decisions that affect our lives was solidified in the first three words of the Constitution: "We, the People."

For two centuries, those words have inspired people around the world, even though the history of the United States is admittedly filled with many deep injustices, starting with the treatment of the land's original inhabitants. In addition, many of those Founding Fathers enslaved people even as they fought for their own liberty. The nation they helped create has weathered many difficulties and crises, including a civil war, a great depression, and two world wars, without surrendering democracy to a Strongman.

So for many of us today, democracy is a matter of fact. A great number of people take those democratic ideals for granted. That may be one reason so many Americans fail to vote or make their voices heard. They prefer to sit on the sidelines instead of actively participating. But democracy is not a spectator sport. It requires work, participation, and sometimes sacrifice. And it can be very fragile. Democracy can die quickly. And that is where we begin.

DEMOCRACY IN FLAMES

The Reichstag, home of the German legislature in Berlin.
[Wikimedia Commons]

If democracy is foolish enough to give us free railway passes and salaries, that is its problem. . . . We are coming neither as friends or neutrals. We come as enemies! As the wolf attacks the sheep, so come we.

—Joseph Goebbels, Propaganda Minister of Nazi Germany, 1933–45

• • •

BERLIN, GERMANY

FEBRUARY 27, 1933

ON A COLD NIGHT in Germany's capital, a university student was walking home from the library. As he passed the majestic building that housed the German parliament, he heard the sound of glass breaking inside and reported this to a police officer making his rounds.

A few minutes later, a typesetter at the newspaper run by the powerful Nazi Party reported seeing a man with a lit torch moving inside the same building—the massive Reichstag. At nearly the same time, a man wearing military boots and a black coat entered a Berlin police station to make an anonymous report that the Reichstag was on fire. Within minutes of this report, the glow of flames could be seen through the Reichstag's towering glass dome. As fire brigades fought the blaze, an explosion rocked the building.

Top leaders of the German government soon raced to the scene of the burning building. First to arrive was Hermann Göring, a member of the Nazi Party who was the interior minister of the German state of Prussia. Next, a black limousine

The window that German authorities said Marinus van der Lubbe used to enter the Reichstag to set the fire. [Wikimedia Commons]

pulled up, carrying the recently appointed chancellor of Germany, Adolf Hitler, and his chief of propaganda, Joseph Goebbels. After surveying the scene, Hitler began shouting that he knew who was responsible for the fire. "There will be no mercy now," Chancellor Hitler vowed. "Every Communist official will be shot where he is found. The Communist deputies must be hanged this very night!"

Even as Hitler raged in what has been described as near-hysteria, a suspect was already in custody. Police had arrested Marinus van der Lubbe, a twenty-four-year-old mason from the Netherlands. Naked to the waist and sweating heavily when captured, Lubbe told the police he had been a member of the Dutch Communist Party's youth organization. Investigators said he soon confessed to setting the fire, determined to make a "defiant protest" against the conditions of the working class.

But did he really do it?

To this day, mysteries about the Reichstag fire remain unsolved. Was it really part of a Communist plot? Or had someone else staged it? Who was the anonymous man in the black coat who reported the fire? Had the Nazis orchestrated the incident to create a national emergency where there was none? Was it all a ploy to falsely paint the Communists in a bad light,

The Reichstag fire. [National Archives]

considering the threat they posed to Hitler and the Nazi Party?

The Nazi press immediately described the fire as the work of the Communists and a signal to begin a general uprising. Yet historians are not certain that this account of events is true, and the origins of the fire remain unclear. True or not, Hitler convinced Germans that his bold actions had saved the nation. The known facts are important to show how a dictator comes to power and how quickly democracy can die.

On this fateful night in 1933, Adolf Hitler was not some self-appointed despot who had taken control of Germany at the head of an army. In 1932, Hitler had run for the presidency of Germany, finishing second to Paul von Hindenburg and raising his profile in the nation. Germany's elected president and a revered war hero, Hindenburg then appointed Hitler to the post of Germany's chancellor on January 30, 1933. Under the German Constitution, the chancellor held great authority, similar to the prime minister of Great Britain. The aging President Hindenburg had offered the post to Adolf Hitler in light of his growing popularity and fears of the Communist Party. Hitler needed little persuasion to seize Germany's reins of power.

Born out of the ashes of its defeat in World War I, the German republic was a modern democracy. The kaiser, the ruler of the old German Empire, had given up his throne in the last days of the war, and the provisional government held elections for a constitutional assembly in 1919—elections in which women had the right to vote, a right U.S. women would not be guaranteed for nearly two more years. The assembly met in Weimar and drafted a new constitution based on the systems of both the

Adolf Hitler in March 1933, two months after being appointed chancellor by President Hindenburg (in uniform). [Wikimedia Commons]

United States and Great Britain, two of the victorious Allies, which had defeated Germany.

The Weimar constitution specified the equality of men and women and included protections for individual freedoms similar to those guaranteed in the U.S. Bill of Rights, including protections for laborers that were not granted to American workers. With guarantees of religious freedom, Germany's new constitution created a tolerant atmosphere, attracting Jewish people from Poland and Russia.

The individual protections and political rights did not stop there. Under this constitution, the Communist Party was a legal group, mostly representing the unemployed, the working classes, and the poorest Germans. Germany had been hit hard by four years of war. Allied blockades had limited some food and medical supplies, and Germany suffered horrific war casualties and the effects of the deadly Spanish flu, which killed four hundred thousand Germans. By the war's end in 1918, the country was in tatters. With few jobs, a generation of young men wiped out or crippled, and food being rationed, a dark, desperate mood was spreading. The Communists, whose ultimate goal was to overthrow the existing economic and political order, offered a stark choice to angry, hopeless people who saw no future.

After the war, Germany's economy was crippled. Inflation—the rapid increase in the cost of goods and services—made German money almost worthless.

Imagine going to buy a pair of jeans that cost fifty dollars when you see them in the shop window. But when you get to the cash register, you are told they now cost one million dollars. This was happening in a time when there were no credit cards or ATMs. German people actually had to push money in wheelbarrows in order to shop.

George Grosz, a German artist who lived through this period, later told how difficult it was to purchase food: "One had to buy quickly because a rabbit, for example, might cost two million marks more by the time it took to walk into the store. A few million marks meant nothing, really. It was just that it meant more lugging. The packages of money needed to buy the smallest item had long since become too heavy for trouser pockets.

A German voter slip from 1936 that reads, "I gave my Voice [vote] to the Führer!" [Wikimedia Commons]

They weighed many pounds. . . . People had to start carting their money around in wagons and knapsacks. I used a knapsack."

While the German economy had improved somewhat in the later 1920s, things unraveled with the Wall Street stock market crash of October 1929. Germany was hit hard by the shock-waves created by what is known as "Black Friday." By some estimates of the day, more than 14 percent of the working population was out of work. Just as Americans suffered during the Great Depression, many German people were devastated. Milk and other basics were rationed, and there was a grim mood. The economic hardships crippled the government as political parties from all sides jockeyed for power. But none had the strength to form a majority government that could answer the country's problems. A power vacuum had been created, opening the way for a Strongman to rise on a platform of making Germany great again. And one man did.

Adolf Hitler and his Nazi Party blamed many of the country's woes on the 1919 Treaty of Versailles, which had severely punished Germany after World War I. In fiery speeches that brought audiences to a frenzy, Hitler blamed Germany's problems on "backstabbers," the politicians who had accepted the harsh treaty. Playing passionately on German patriotism, Hitler raged not only at the nations that won the war but also at international bankers and Jewish people in general. Hitler appealed to a deep strain of anti-Semitism, a very ancient prejudice against Jews. As he made scapegoats of various groups, blaming them for his country's woes, Hitler's popularity continued to soar. In 1930, the Nazi Party became the second largest in the Reichstag. It was a "political earthquake," says Ian Kershaw. "The Nazi bandwagon was rolling."

Communism—which argues for a classless society in which property and the means of production are owned and governed in common—was also squarely in Hitler's sights. With the Reichstag in flames, Hitler had the excuse he needed to target one of his chief political rivals. The Communists had tried to destroy the Reichstag, Hitler claimed, as part of their plan for a violent revolution to take over Germany. The fact that Marinus van der Lubbe was a Communist clinched his argument.

To many despairing but wary Germans, the fear of Communism was real. They knew about the deadly Bolshevik Revolution, which had bloodied Russia and led to the merciless killing of Russia's ruler, the czar, and his family in July 1918. Germans were terrified that a similar uprising might sweep their country. Religion also influenced German attitudes toward Communism. An overwhelmingly Christian country—about two-thirds were Protestant, one-third Catholic, and barely 1 percent Jewish—many Germans dreaded Communism's atheism.

Urged on by Hitler the next day, President Hindenburg issued a decree "for the protection of the people and state." This emergency order was sweeping and repressive, but perfectly legal. The Reichstag Fire Decree erased many of the freedoms cemented in the Weimar constitution and gave the government full power to arrest and jail opponents without specific charges, dissolve political groups, and control Germany's press. Police began making mass arrests. Nazi storm troopers went on a tear, scooping up political opponents and beating them in basements and warehouses. Many fearful Germans welcomed the moves. "The violence and repression were widely popular," biographer Ian Kershaw notes. "The 'emergency decree' that took away all personal liberties and established the platform for dictatorship was warmly welcomed."

To this day, there is no certainty that Communists were responsible for the burning of the Reichstag. The young Dutchman, Marinus van der Lubbe, was tried and convicted of arson and of attempting to overthrow the government. He was executed in January 1934, but there are still deep suspicions that he was simply a scapegoat, brought to the scene by Nazi agents who had actually set multiple fires. Four other Communists who were tried at the same time for their alleged role in setting the Reichstag fire were all acquitted for lack of evidence.

But the damage was done. Barely three weeks after the Reichstag Fire Decree, Hitler further tightened his grip. Detaining Communist and leftist members of the legislature in so-called protective custody, the Nazis intimidated the rest of parliament into passing the Law to Remedy the Distress of the People and the Reich, also known as the Enabling Act. The act gave the Reich government, under Hitler, the power to issue laws without approval of the legislature or regard for the constitution—effectively making Hitler Germany's undisputed ruler.

Now armed with nearly unlimited power to jail political opponents and shut down newspapers, Adolf Hitler established a one-party state in Germany. Eventually, that boundless authority led to the Holocaust and World War II. It all happened so quickly. And it was all perfectly constitutional.

As one German journalist later wrote, "First the Reichstag burned, then the books, then the synagogues. Then Germany began to burn, [then] England, France, and Russia."

German democracy died in the Reichstag flames. Just as Plato had predicted two thousand years earlier, tyranny had defeated democracy.

BEFORE THE COMMON ERA (BCE)

ca. 594 **ATHENS**: The statesman Solon lays groundwork for democracy.

509 **ROME**: The Roman Republic is founded.

ca. 508 **ATHENS**: Cleisthenes introduces reforms that establish democracy.

462–458 **ATHENS**: Pericles strengthens democratic institutions in the Greek city-state.

ca. 460–ca. 320 **ATHENS**: A period of direct citizen democracy in Athens.

ca. 450 **ROME**: The Law of the Twelve Tables is formally posted in the Roman Forum so that everyone can become familiar with the legal code.

322 **ATHENS**: Athenian democracy ends when Macedonia defeats Athenian forces and ends the city's self-rule.

149–146 **ROME**: Roman armies destroy rival Carthage in North Africa in the Third Punic War, and the Roman Republic emerges as the dominant power in the Mediterranean world.

63 **ROME**: Catiline plots to overthrow the republic.

46 **ROME**: Julius Caesar becomes dictator for a term of ten years.

ca. Feb. 44 **ROME**: The senate names Caesar dictator in perpetuum.

March 15, 44 **ROME**: Caesar is assassinated.

27 **ROME**: Octavian, Caesar's heir, becomes first Roman emperor, taking the name Augustus.

COMMON ERA (CE)

1215 **ENGLAND:** King John signs the Magna Carta, which subjects monarchs to the rule of law and outlines the liberties of free men.

1295	**ENGLAND**: King Edward I calls the Model Parliament to raise money for war; the gathering includes commoners and is considered the first representative parliament.
1517	**EUROPE**: The Protestant Reformation begins.
1535	**SWITZERLAND**: Inspired by Protestant reformers, the city of Geneva ousts its ruling bishop and becomes a free republic.
1688–89	**ENGLAND**: In the Glorious Revolution, Catholic King James II is overthrown in favor of his Protestant daughter Mary and her husband, William of Orange; Parliament passes a Bill of Rights.
1776	**UNITED STATES**: The Declaration of Independence is signed.
1787	**UNITED STATES**: The U.S. Constitution is drafted.
1789	**FRANCE**: The French Revolution begins.
1791–1804	**HAITI**: Enslaved people revolt against slaveholders and colonial power during the Haitian Revolution.
1848	**EUROPE**: A wave of revolutions calling for democratic reforms sweeps across the continent, including France, the Netherlands, the German states, Italy, and Austria.
1861	**RUSSIA**: Serfs are emancipated in the Russian Empire.
March 17, **1861**	**ITALY**: The Risorgimento leads to the establishment of a parliamentary constitutional monarchy in the new Kingdom of Italy.
1861–1865	**UNITED STATES**: The Civil War leads to the Thirteenth Amendment to the Constitution, abolishing slavery.
Feb. 12, **1912**	**CHINA**: The last Qing emperor abdicates four months after military officers lead a revolt and proclaim the Republic of China.
1914–1918	**WORLD WAR I** is fought.
1917	**RUSSIA**: The Russian Revolution overthrows the czar.

"LET ARMS YIELD TO THE TOGA"

George Washington, depicted in Roman robes, in an 1841 statue modeled on an ancient statue of the Greek god Zeus.
[Wikimedia Commons]

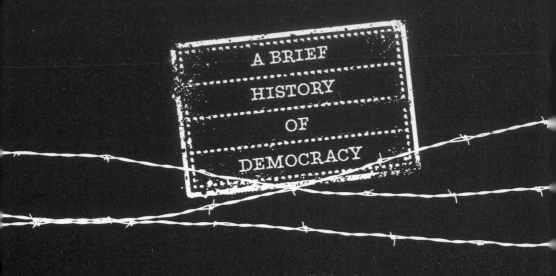

A BRIEF HISTORY OF DEMOCRACY

It is true that we are called a democracy,
for the administration is in the hands
of the many and not of the few.

—**Thucydides,** Funeral Speech of Pericles

• • •

Let arms yield to the toga.

—**Cicero,** *Di Officilis*

• • •

It is requisite the government be so constituted as one
man need not be afraid of another.

—**Montesquieu,** *The Spirit of Laws*

• • •

The evils we experience flow from
the excess of democracy.

—**Elbridge Gerry,** *Debates in the Federal Convention of 1787*

• • •

DEMOCRACY. It is a common word, used almost every day in the United States and elsewhere around the world. Depending on who's using it, *democracy* can mean majority rule, rule by the people, or the right to self-govern. It usually signals the promise of equality and liberty. And it is almost always viewed positively.

But perhaps surprisingly, the word *democracy* does not appear in either the Declaration of Independence or the U.S. Constitution. And to some of America's Founding Fathers, democracy was a dangerous idea, just one small step removed from mob rule. *Federalist Paper* Number 51, written in support of the Constitution and attributed to either Alexander Hamilton, who became America's first treasury secretary, or James Madison, who became America's fourth president, says, "If men were angels, no government would be necessary. . . . It is of great importance in a republic, not only to guard the society against the oppression of its rulers; but to guard one part of the society against the injustice of the other part."

During the Constitutional Convention debates, Hamilton, now of Broadway fame, had proposed a permanent legislature, arguing, "The people are turbulent and changing; they seldom judge or determine right. . . . Can a democratic assembly, who annually revolve in the mass of the people, be supposed steadily to pursue the public good?" Elbridge Gerry, another delegate to the Constitutional Convention, said, "The evils we experience flow from the excess of democracy." Like many of the men who helped write the Constitution, Gerry feared that a majority making decisions would not necessarily lead to fair or good policies or laws. Many of the framers of the Constitution did not believe that most citizens were qualified by education or their religious training to make sound decisions.

These men feared a pure democracy in which "one man, one vote" carried the day, creating a tyranny by majority. They recognized a fundamental truth: simply because an idea is popular does not make it just or desirable. For instance, a class might vote to have a pizza party by majority rule. That is basically fair. But if the majority decided that some of the students are not allowed to eat the pizza, that is not fair.

Many times in American history large majorities have favored certain systems or policies, such as slavery, segregation, or denying the vote to women, which eventually were changed through constitutional amendments and court decisions.

Working secretly in the summer of 1787, the Constitution's framers drafted a plan for a national government based on the idea of "representative democracy"—in which officials are chosen in elections to act for the people, and presumably to carry out their will. Such men—and they were all men—would possess the wisdom to do the right thing. At least, that is the theory. The rules saying who could vote would be left to the individual states. In effect, however, the right to vote was largely limited to white, male property holders, which was gradually expanded to include most white men over twenty-one. But, of course, for many years women, African Americans, and Native Americans were still excluded from U.S. elections.

Democracy comes from the Greek words *demos*—"the people"—and *kratie*—"power" or "authority." In its most ancient sense, democracy meant that people had the power. In the ancient world of Athens more than 2,500 years ago, democracy stood in contrast to *aristocracy*, from the Greek word *aristos*— "best of its kind, noblest, bravest, most virtuous." Only later did *aristocracy* evolve to mean, as it commonly does now, rule by the wealthy, an upper class, or hereditary ranks of nobility.

So we begin with the "cradle of democracy," ancient Greece and, more precisely, Athens. More than two thousand years ago in this Greek city-state, an idea that would transform the world first took root and slowly flowered. Although the Greek experiment in democracy eventually disappeared, it gave birth to a concept that would not die.

By about 600 BCE, Athens had emerged in ancient Greece as the leading city-state, or *polis*. Like other Greek city-states, Athens had long been ruled by powerful and wealthy men. From four principal families, the men of Athens began to meet on a hill in an assembly called the Areopagus and were called *archons*, or chief magistrates. The word *archon*, in turn, gives us two other familiar political terms: **monarchy** is from the Greek *monarkhia*—for "absolute rule"—literally "ruling of one," from *monos,* "alone," and *arkhein,* "to rule." Therefore, a monarchy establishes rule or government by a single person. The word **oligarchy** comes from *oligarkhia*, with the root *oligos* meaning "few, small, little." In other words, an oligarchy means rule or government by the few.

By 621 BCE, Athens was a wealthy port city and trading center in the Mediterranean world, and a power struggle took shape. The unequal distribution of wealth in its many

Athenian men met to vote on the Areopagus, a hill named for Ares, the god of war. Areopagus was also the name of the assembly. [Wikimedia Commons]

forms—land, trade, property, and enslaved people—has often been at the heart of history's conflicts. What is now called "income inequality" has caused strife for a very long time. The "haves," the wealthy and most powerful, want to keep what they have and acquire even more. The "have-nots" want what they don't have.

The Greek philosopher Plato identified this problem in *Laws* (ca. 360 BCE), when he said, "In a state which is desirous of being saved from the greatest of all plagues—not faction, but rather distraction—*there should exist among the citizens neither extreme poverty nor, again, excessive wealth, for both are productive of both these evils.* Now the legislator should determine what is to be the limit of poverty or wealth." (Emphasis added.)

Plato thought the ideal government should set those limits

to ensure a just society. In fact, one of his ancestors, an archon named Solon, had set out to resolve the city's sometimes violent conflicts over wealth and power around 594 BCE. Solon's reforms permitted any free person to vote in the assembly. Perhaps even more important, he suggested the elimination of debts that sometimes allowed people to be enslaved, and he opened Athenian democracy up to more people. He also expanded the definition of *citizen* to include men who were not of the wealthiest class, such as merchants and even ordinary laborers—although women and slaves still had no right to vote—altering the lines of power in Athens.

Solon's reforms may have been unique, even revolutionary in the ancient world, but they fell far short of ideal. After some time, simmering political disputes boiled over until a despot or tyrant—a type of ruler with absolute power—took control. *Tyrant* comes from the Greek *tyrannos*, meaning "lord, master, sovereign, absolute ruler unlimited by law or constitution." In Athens, a successful military leader named Peisistratus seized power from the people three separate times from 560 to his death in 527 BCE.

Attempting to fix the system, another Athenian archon named Cleisthenes proposed further democratic reforms in 508 BCE. Later called the Father of Athenian Democracy, he broke up the four most powerful Athenian clans by creating new voting rules based on where people lived rather than what clan they belonged to. Cleisthenes thus weakened the hereditary power of the largest, wealthiest families, which led to a much wider participation in the public affairs of Athens.

As it evolved, the democratic system of Athens was based largely on a direct assembly. Meeting at least once a month in an open-air space, the assembly was a form of "direct democracy," in which men voted on decisions with a simple show of hands. Leaders were chosen by lot—picked at random—and served for a year. Thousands of men voting in the open air sounds like an unwieldy way to run a city. But in large measure, it worked. To be clear, a free person meant free male; women and enslaved people had no voice in this Greek democracy.

But Athens soon faced a much greater threat than a homegrown tyrant: Persia, one of the world's first superpowers. Based in what is today Iran and Iraq, Persia's empire stretched from the Indus River to the Aegean Sea, and in 492 BCE it set its sights on the Greek peninsula. For nearly half a century, the Greek city-states fended off the Persians in a series of intermittent Greco-Persian wars. Several legendary battles in this long, costly conflict—at Thermopylae, Marathon, and an Athenian naval victory at Salamis—are still counted among the most significant battles in Western history. While the Persians burned Athens in 480 BCE, the ultimate Greek triumph ensured the survival of Greece, and the cultural and political structure of Athens. Since Greece survived, so did democracy. For much of the next century, from 460 to 320 BCE, Athens and its democracy would be the leading power in the Greek world.

However, the victory over Persia didn't bring much peace to Greece. Athens was soon fighting Sparta, its most powerful rival *polis*, in the Peloponnesian War. Led by a general named Pericles, Athens maintained its democratic system through

Persians destroy the temples on the Acropolis of Athens. [Wikimedia Commons]

wartime, best exemplified in a speech given by Pericles in honor of Athenians who died fighting in the war. An Athenian general and historian named Thucydides recorded it:

"Our form of government does not enter into rivalry with the institutions of others. We do not copy our neighbors, but are an example to them. It is true that we are called a democracy, for the administration is in the hands of the many and not

Pericles's funeral oration. [Wikimedia Commons]

of the few. But while the law secures equal justice to all alike in their private disputes, the claim of excellence is also recognized; and when a citizen is in any way distinguished, he is preferred to the public service, not as a matter of privilege, but as the reward of merit. Neither is poverty a bar, but a man may benefit his country whatever be the obscurity of his condition."

Is this what Pericles *actually* said? Some historians wonder. They also ask whether Athens lived up to such high ideals. There is little doubt that the inspirational words ascribed to Pericles spoke to the basic dream of democracy—power shared by many, along with justice, equality, and merit. One phrase in that speech, in particular, is now considered a fundamental tenet in the U.S. government and legal systems. The words EQUAL JUSTICE UNDER LAW—which capture the spirit of the democratic ideal that Pericles had offered in ancient Greece—are engraved over the entrance to the U.S. Supreme Court building.

Through years of the ongoing Peloponnesian Wars, and a mysterious plague that took the life of Pericles and may have killed an estimated quarter of the population, Athens gradually lost much of its power. When King Philip II of neighboring Macedonia conquered most of Greece around 338 BCE, the experiment with democracy in Athens was fading. Athens

The west pediment of the Supreme Court building, built in 1935, in Washington, D.C. [Wikimedia Commons]

and all of Greece became part of the sprawling empire created by Philip's son, Alexander the Great. Although the Greeks ruled themselves and Alexander spread Greek culture across his empire, the democratic ideals of Pericles were not what Alexander took with him. When Alexander died, the vestiges of democracy in Athens died with him, as Alexander's successor ended the city's self-rule. Democracy had fallen to a Strongman.

Around the same time that Athenian democracy fell to a despot, another form of democratic rule was rising in an emerging Mediterranean power on the boot-shaped peninsula of Italy. In the legend of Rome's foundation, the twin brothers Romulus

Considered the symbol of Rome, the life-size Capitoline Wolf statue depicts the she-wolf nursing the twins Romulus and Remus. Mussolini gave the statue to Japan, Italy's wartime ally. [Wikimedia Commons]

and Remus were the mortal sons of the mythical war god Mars. Seeing the infant boys as a threat, their great uncle the king had them thrown into the Tiber River. Rescued from drowning and suckled by a she-wolf, the twins were later raised by a shepherd. Eventually, they set out to found their own city, but the twins fought over the location, and Romulus killed his brother. He named the city Rome, after himself, and became its first king.

According to Livy's *History of Rome*, a first-century account, the legendary Romulus was followed by a string of Roman kings. Eventually, the Romans replaced their monarch with two consuls, or magistrates, who served together for a year and were responsible for leading Rome's armies in battle. This was the seed of something extraordinary because the consuls were elected, whereas past kings had been appointed by a small council. It didn't happen in a sudden flash of lightning, but over time, the Romans developed a form of democracy far more influential than the Greek model.

What they created was the first known representative government in the Western world, a **republic**. In **representative democracies**, people vote for people to serve on councils, whose members then vote on laws, as opposed to a direct democracy as the Athenians practiced it.

The word *republic* comes from the Latin words *res*, "affair, matter," and *publica*, "public." While the traditional birth date of the Roman Republic is given as 509 BCE, clouds of legend have obscured the facts. In her book *SPQR*, historian Mary Beard offers a lengthy time line in which the republic in Rome was "born slowly over a period of decades, if not centuries. It was reinvented many times over."

As the Roman Republic evolved, power flowed gradually from the consuls to the **Senate**, or the "council of elders." The word *senate* comes from the Latin word *senex*. The Latin root *sen*, for "old" or "old man," also gives us such words in English as *senior* and *senile*. During Rome's monarchy, a form of the Senate may have existed as a council of advisers to the king. Under the republic, the Senate became Rome's decision-making body and provided the republic's enduring symbol, SPQR, which stood for Senatus Populusque Romanus (Senate and People of Rome).

To be clear, "people of Rome" did not mean everybody. As in Athens, the city's citizens were sharply divided into two main classes. At the top of the ladder were the **patricians**, the families descended from the senators of the old Roman kings. Next came the **plebeians**, members of the general population who did not possess the wealth and influence of the patricians. But all plebeians were not created equal, and there were many distinctions of class and wealth. Within the plebeian ranks was the large group of Romans called the **proletariat**—mostly working-class people and laborers with no property. Although Roman women of some classes were considered citizens, they could not vote. Then at the very bottom rung of Roman society was the city's massive enslaved population—usually people taken as prisoners of war—which included not only common laborers but also artists, musicians, teachers, secretaries, and other skilled professionals who contributed to Rome's emergence as a great power. Like the enslaved of Athens, Roman slaves had no right to citizenship.

The contest between patrician and plebeian was no even match, and as a result, vast inequality arose in Rome. "In the early years of the Republic, the patricians held and controlled all the political and social power of the state," Robert Hughes writes in his history of Rome. "Only patricians could be elected to any office, including the all-important senatorships. Only they could serve as priests. The plebeians, by contrast, were excluded from religious colleges, magistracies, and as a rule, from the Senate; early on, they were also forbidden to marry patricians. With lawmaking and religion in patrician control, what was left for plebeians?"

The answer is the army. While the Roman army's generals were often patricians, the lower-ranking commanders— centurions, who led one hundred soldiers—and most troops were plebeians, who by 287 BCE had gained full and equal status in Roman political life. As Roman soldiers, they were not only paid but also expected to share in the booty, or spoils of war—which could mean captured land, property, possessions, and, most of all, people. Trading and selling captured enemies as slaves made great fortunes, allowing some plebeians to rise up the social ladder.

Largely on the strength of its armies, Rome grew from about ten thousand square kilometers in 326 BCE to nearly two million square kilometers by 50 BCE. "The city on the Tiber," says Robert Hughes, "was well on its way to ruling the known world."

As the republic flourished through wars, invasions, intrigues, and slave rebellions, so did corruption. In the first century BCE, Rome was becoming more wealthy and, as the city's population approached one million, more difficult to manage. Soon, Roman democracy was put up for sale.

A seat in the Senate became the way to gain power and wealth. Roman politicians began to openly buy votes and use gang violence to intimidate their rivals for office. Men who could provide free food and the best entertainment in the gladiator spectacles that Romans loved often won elections. This practice was known as "bread and circuses." But doling out loaves of bread and staging contests in which men fought one another to the death could not mask the filthy streets, food shortages, and unemployment making the city chaotic.

Despite the enormous wealth flowing into the city, Rome was plagued by crime, shabby buildings that often caught fire, and widespread hunger. While enslaved servants carried patricians and wealthy plebeians around Rome in elaborate chairs or beds, called litters, common people were forced to walk through the city's muddy, sewage-filled streets.

Dodging the pigs and other animals wandering in the crowded, narrow alleyways, ordinary Romans had to be alert to someone tossing a chamber pot's contents out an open window. Seeing the vast riches separating the patricians from everyone else—another example of "income inequality"—many Romans were eager for a Strongman who would tear down the existing order and clean up the Senate.

What they wanted was a **dictator**. That is another Roman

word whose meaning has changed. Early on, whenever there was a military or internal crisis, the Roman Senate appointed a dictator—a temporary magistrate who was given absolute power for six months.

Another brand of dictator appeared in Rome in 49 BCE. From an old patrician family, Julius Caesar was a successful politician and even more successful general whose victories in the Gallic Wars made him a Roman hero. Caesar's popularity was growing, and the Senate worried about his power. The Senate ordered Caesar to surrender command of his troops.

Under the republic, Roman law did not permit a general to bring an army across the Rubicon—a shallow river marking the northern boundary of Italy. But a defiant Caesar marched his Thirteenth Legion across the river in 49 BCE. According to Roman author Suetonius, Caesar uttered the famous phrase *iacta alea est*—"the die is now cast," meaning he was taking his chances as he tossed the dice, like moving around the Monopoly board. Even today, the expression "crossing the Rubicon" means making a highly risky decision without any chance of going back.

To the Senate, Caesar's roll of the dice was an act of treason. He would be either arrested or destroyed. His decision led to four years of civil war. While supporters in Rome rushed to join Caesar, another general, Pompey, was directed to oppose him. But Pompey's superior numbers were defeated in 48 BCE at the Battle of Pharsalus in northern Greece; Pompey sought to escape to Egypt, where he was murdered and decapitated. Caesar's chief rival's severed head was sent to Rome.

Caesar continued his battle against Romans who opposed him, but that opposition weakened as he added more military victories and rewarded his loyal soldiers and accommodating politicians with the spoils of his military success. In 46 BCE, he was named dictator for ten years. Two years later, in 44 BCE, his title and term were changed to *dictator in perpetuum*—literally, a dictator forever. Democracy had passed to a despot.

His power growing, Caesar began to be identified as a living god, and his image was placed on Roman coins, breaking a Roman taboo against depicting living people on coins. The Roman calendar was revised, and the month previously called Quintilis was renamed "Julius," the English "July," in his honor.

A group of senators who supposedly wanted to restore the republic conspired to kill him. On the Ides of March—March 15—Julius Caesar was stabbed to death in the Senate. The scene was immortalized centuries later by Shakespeare's play *Julius Caesar*.

The assassination of Julius Caesar painted by William Holmes Sullivan.
[Wikimedia Commons]

In the chaos and civil war that followed the murder, Caesar's allies attempted to replace him as Rome's ruler. Among the competing rivals, Caesar's onetime friend Mark Anthony was eventually defeated by Octavian, Julius Caesar's nephew and adopted son. Octavian later took the name Caesar Augustus, and under him Rome was ruled as an empire, not a republic.

The rise and fall of the Roman Republic is so significant in U.S. history because many of the founding generation of American politicians looked to Rome as an ideal form of government. They held a highly idealized notion of the Roman Republic as a collection of great men who ruled wisely. George Washington's favorite play was *Cato*, a 1713 tragedy about a Roman senator who defied Julius Caesar. Washington had *Cato* performed for the troops at Valley Forge.

During the revolutionary era, American patriots used Roman pseudonyms to hide their identities. Samuel Adams used Cedant Arma Togae (Let Arms Yield to the Toga) on a 1768 essay protesting the British standing army. The phrase was from Cicero, a hero of the Roman Republic, who meant that military power, or arms, should be controlled by the elected representatives, the Roman senators who wore togas.

In Boston on March 5, 1775, Dr. Joseph Warren dressed as Cicero, wearing a white toga over his suit to make a speech at Old South Church. Dr. Warren's toga wasn't part of some amusing patriot masquerade party. He was one of the Sons of Liberty, a secret group of American patriots who organized the resistance to British rule. Like many of the founding generation, Warren thought the Roman Republic represented the ideal government: wise, noble men leading the people with a sense of virtue. It was certainly idealistic if woefully inaccurate, considering the levels of corruption and political infighting that took place in Rome.

While the U.S. Constitution was being debated in 1787 and 1788 before its ultimate ratification, prominent politicians James Madison, Alexander Hamilton, and John Jay jointly used the name Publius as a pseudonym in their defense of the Constitution in the *Federalist Papers*. Other men who wrote to either support or oppose the Constitution signed anonymously under such famous Roman names as Brutus, Cato, and Cincinnatus.

"The founders considered the Roman Republic a prototype for their new nation and the Roman Empire a cautionary lesson of potential failure," explains Hope Grossman of George Washington University. "Classical depictions of Roman civil wars produced the archetypal republican heroes and power hungry villains that became common references in American political rhetoric in the late eighteenth and early nineteenth centuries."

That is one reason George Washington was memorialized in 1841 via a large marble statue modeled on a classical figure of the Greek god Zeus. It depicts a seated Washington, bare chested, wearing sandals, and draped in a toga. His right arm points toward heaven. He cradles a sheathed sword, hilt forward, symbolizing Washington turning power over to the people. As Cicero would have put it, arms had yielded to the toga.

America's form of democracy emerged after centuries

of powerful changes and upheaval, particularly in Western Europe. The Age of Discovery had introduced Europeans to new worlds. The Protestant Reformation had weakened the power of the pope as Christianity's single unquestioned leader. Gutenberg's printing press created an "information revolution" as the Bible and other books became more available, gradually spreading literacy and eventually allowing the general population to be better educated and informed. Microscopes and telescopes changed the view of the heavens and revealed invisible worlds, and scientists like Isaac Newton, with his laws of physics, questioned the order of nature. In this period, called the "Age of Enlightenment," many European thinkers began to introduce radical ideas about human rights and liberties.

The beginnings of the Industrial Revolution in the mid-eighteenth century also reshaped the ways wealth—and the power it brought—were acquired. No longer did a fortune rely on inherited titles and property. Bankers and wool merchants, many of whom were self-made men, were becoming the new princes. The supremacy of religious leaders and monarchs ruling with "divine right of kings" was shoved aside. A new era saw declarations of basic human liberties overturning the old order. The concept that all people were entitled to "life, liberty, and the pursuit of happiness"—inspired by English philosopher John Locke's 1689 ideas—were still fairly startling notions in 1776.

"All this was breathtakingly novel," writes Akhil Reed Amar in his biography of the Constitution. "In 1787, democratic self-government existed almost nowhere on earth. Kings, emperors, czars, princes, sultans, moguls, feudal lords, and tribal chiefs held sway across the globe. . . . The vaunted English Constitution that American colonists had grown up admiring prior to the struggle for independence was an imprecise hodgepodge of institutions, enactments, cases, usages, maxims, procedures, and principles that had accreted and evolved over many centuries. . . . Before the American Revolution, no people had ever explicitly voted on their own written Constitution."

By embracing shared powers under a republic, the framers of the Constitution embarked in 1787 on a bold experiment in government. But their idealism was tempered by their fears— of an unruly mob on one hand or a tyrant on the other—as well as their prejudices against women, Native Americans, and black people, who were not afforded equal rights.

That was why they were so cautious about giving unlimited power to an executive they called the **president**—another word with the Latin roots—*prae*, "before," and *sedeo*, "sit"—meaning "to sit before." Instead, they created a system of carefully calculated checks and balances to maintain equal strength among the three branches of their new government. In this system, the guiding concept was the separation of powers, a fundamental idea found in the writings of the French philosopher Montesquieu. In 1748, Montesquieu had written, "It is requisite the government be so constituted as one man need not be afraid of another."

The influence of Montesquieu and other Enlightenment thinkers led to the shaping of democracy in America. Adapting concepts Montesquieu had laid out, the framers set up the new

U.S. government with three parts: legislative, executive, and judicial. The legislature, or Congress, would be divided into two houses. The upper house, the Senate—named after its Roman predecessor—would have two senators from each state, regardless of the state's population. The lower house, the House of Representatives, would be based on each state's population, meaning each state elects a certain number of representatives in proportion to its total population.

At the same time, fear of an excess of democracy and mob rule led to other built-in safeguards. Under the original Constitution, U.S. senators were elected by state legislatures, not directly by the people. (That changed with ratification of the Seventeenth Amendment in 1913.) And of course, the president would not be elected by a direct popular vote. Instead, each state would receive electors equal to the number of seats they held in Congress—what is now referred to as the Electoral College.

For most of American presidential history, popular votes and electoral votes have aligned, with a few exceptions. In 1824, the House elected John Quincy Adams, choosing him over Andrew Jackson, who had won the most popular votes in what had been a strange four-way race. In 1876, Rutherford B. Hayes was made president despite Samuel Tilden winning the popular vote. In 1888, Benjamin Harrison won the presidency even though Grover Cleveland won the popular vote. And two times in recent American presidential elections—in 2000 and 2016—the winner of the popular vote lost out to the winner in the electoral vote. This is an outcome designed by men who feared direct elections over two hundred years ago. It was also a system in which the framers, including James Madison, the Father of the Constitution, cemented the legal role of slavery in the founding of the republic. Like fellow Virginians and future presidents Washington, Jefferson, and Monroe, Madison enslaved people who had no more rights than a farm animal.

Still, since its revolutionary birth in 1776, the United States has weathered many divisive periods. The federal republic created under the Constitution in 1789 has seen wars, racial and religious strife, and such profound crises as the Civil War, the Great Depression, and two world wars. But through discord and uncertainty, there has never been an American version of Julius Caesar or of France's Napoleon Bonaparte, two of history's most famous examples of successful generals who overturned republics and seized nearly unlimited powers.

The U.S. system of checks and balances has so far prevented the worst-case scenario. At the same time, the United States has inspired other revolutions and republics. In 1789, France went through its bloody revolution under the banner of *liberté, égalité, fraternité* (liberty, equality, fraternity). The motto was shared in Haiti, the second republic born in the Western Hemisphere, when in 1791 enslaved people on the Caribbean island rose up against the slaveholders in another violent revolution. Both of these rebellions eventually turned into long, violent conflicts.

Despite these setbacks to the idea of people ruling themselves, the nineteenth century saw democracy ascending, if ever so slowly. A wave of revolutions calling for democratic reforms

The Battle of San Domingo, also known as The Battle for Palm Tree Hill, painted in 1845 by January Suchodolski, depicts the fighting during the Haitian Revolution. [Wikimedia Commons]

swept Europe in the middle of the nineteenth century, leading to the emergence of new representative governments—many of them parliamentary constitutional monarchies like that of Great Britain—in the Netherlands, the German states, and Italy, where the monarch still held supreme power.

As the twentieth century opened, democracy seemed to be gaining a stronger foothold in Europe. That came crashing down in August 1914, when all of Europe went to war. Initially, the United States took a neutral stance, but it was eventually drawn into war with Germany. When President Woodrow

Wilson asked for a declaration of war on April 2, 1917, he said, "The world must be made safe for democracy. Its peace must be planted upon the tested foundations of political liberty. . . . We are but one of the champions of the rights of mankind. We shall be satisfied when those rights have been made as secure as the faith and the freedom of nations can make them."

That global conflict, first called the Great War and later to be known as World War I, would be optimistically called "the war to end all wars." But the fighting and death did precious little to make the world safe for democracy. Instead, it sowed the seeds for the rise of a new generation of Strongmen around the world.

TIME LINE—
THE LIFE OF BENITO MUSSOLINI

July 29, **1883** ··· Benito Mussolini is born in Predappio, a small town in northeastern Italy.

1915-1917 ··· Mussolini serves in World War I.

March **1919** ··· Fasci di Combattimento is formed.

May **1921** ··· Mussolini is elected to Chamber of Deputies.

Oct. 28, **1922** ··· The Fascists march on Rome.

Oct. 30, **1922** ··· Italian king names Mussolini prime minister.

Dec. **1925** ··· Parliament cedes its power to Mussolini, naming him head of government.

June **1934** ··· Mussolini and Hitler meet in Venice.

Oct. **1935** ··· Italy invades Ethiopia (Abyssinia).

1936-1939 ··· Spanish Civil War: Italy sends troops, planes, and other arms to aid the forces led by General Francisco Franco.

May **1938** ··· Hitler makes a weeklong visit to Mussolini in Rome.

Sept. **1938** ··· Mussolini's government revokes civil rights of Italian Jews.

July 10, **1943** ··· The Allied invasion of Italy begins.

July 25, **1943** ··· Mussolini is replaced as prime minister.

April 28, **1945** ··· Mussolini is executed.

April **1946** ··· Mussolini's body is stolen from his unmarked grave; it is later recovered and buried in a crypt in his hometown.

"BELIEVE, OBEY, AND FIGHT"

Benito Mussolini after his appointment as prime minister of Italy in October 1922.
[Wikimedia Commons]

THE STORY OF BENITO MUSSOLINI

Either the government will be given to us or we shall
seize it by marching on Rome.

—**Benito Mussolini**

• • •

If Mussolini would have me taken out and shot tomorrow
morning I would still regard him as a bluff.

—**Ernest Hemingway**

• • •

Then one of them took my arm and looked at my
number and then both laughed still more strongly.
Everyone knows that 174000s are the Italian Jews, the
well-known Italian Jews who arrived two months ago, all
lawyers, all with degrees, who were more than a hundred
and are now only forty; the ones who do not know how
to work, and let their bread be stolen, and are slapped
from the morning to the evening.

—**Primo Levi,** *Survival in Auschwitz*

• • •

ROME, ITALY
OCTOBER 28, 1922

JULIUS CAESAR ENTERED ROME in a blaze of glory, in a chariot, leading his loyal Roman legion.

Benito Mussolini arrived in a sleeper compartment on an overnight train.

It was October 1922 and Mussolini's Blackshirts were converging on Rome from many points around Italy. Not to be confused with the battle-tested Thirteenth Legion that gave Caesar his victory, this ragtag collection included army veterans of the recent war. Some of them brandished pilfered weapons, handed over by sympathetic soldiers and police officers. Even so, the sight was not very intimidating.

"The overall array of weaponry included shotguns, muskets, powder-loaded pistols, golf clubs, scythes, garden hoes, tree roots, table legs, dynamite sticks, dried salt codfish, and an ox's jawbone!" writes historian Blaine Taylor. "Horses, carts, trucks, wagons, bicycles, and even a race car with a machine gun mounted on it were employed for transport . . . while many more moved toward the capital on foot."

This was the March on Rome—a threat to overthrow the

Italian government by Mussolini's Fascist Party. The danger to Italy's government seemed real enough that Prime Minister Luigi Facta proclaimed martial law—the control of a country by the military, usually in response to a temporary emergency, such as a natural disaster or a specific enemy threat.

These Blackshirts were the foot soldiers in Mussolini's Fascist Party, their uniforms modeled on those of the Arditi, an elite army corps that fought in World War I. Some of the men were former members of the Arditi, tough fighters known for their daggers and one-armed salute—a gesture carried over from Rome's storied legions. Many of them had joined Mussolini's party and were fanatically committed to the Fascist creed: "Believe, obey, and fight."

Men of the Italian Arditi during World War I.
[Wikimedia Commons]

Wounded in a training exercise during the Great War, Benito Mussolini had still gained national fame as a persuasive orator and newspaper editor. He understood the power of words and images to shape public opinion. Elected to the Italian parliament's Chamber of Deputies in 1921, Mussolini possessed large political ambitions and a grandiose sense of history and himself. He wanted to control Italy and understood the value of recalling Rome's glorious past.

He knew that the sight of his Blackshirts moving on Rome to seize power and bring order to an Italy racked by political chaos would send a clear message—his army was also "crossing the Rubicon," as Julius Caesar had done. The Blackshirts converging on Rome evoked a past glory that would be welcomed by many unemployed, downtrodden, and disillusioned Italians. The very name **Fascist** was adopted from a symbol of ancient Rome. The fasces, an emblem of a magistrate's power, was typically shown as an ax bound in a bundle of rods. The original Latin word *fascis* meant "bundle."

In the election of May 1921, the Fascists had won thirty-five seats in the legislature, far from enough to lead the nation. Mussolini would have to join other parties in a coalition government, which meant sharing power.

Mussolini clearly had no interest in such a deal, and he declared in September 1922, "Our program is simple. We want to govern Italy."

At dawn on October 28, 1922, the Fascist march was launched in a heavy downpour. As the main force of Blackshirts approached Rome, other Fascists seized telephone

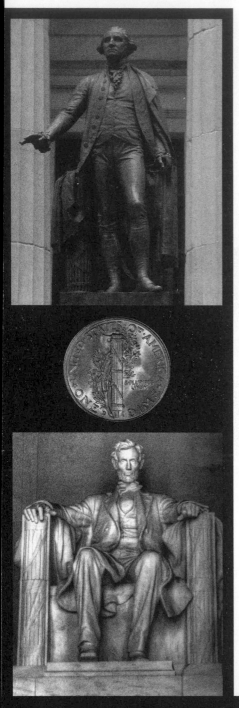

switchboards, telegraph offices, post offices, and government buildings across Italy. The rebellion that the prime minister feared was underway.

What the marchers did not know was that Mussolini, unlike Caesar, was taking no chances as he tossed the dice. Hours away from Rome in Milan, Mussolini waited, barricaded safely inside his newspaper offices to see whether luck was with him. It was.

That same morning Italy's king, Victor Emmanuel III, refused to sign Prime Minister Facta's proclamation of martial law. Mussolini knew he had won the game.

While Italian troops were in place to turn back Mussolini's poorly armed marchers, the timid king had his secretary call Mussolini at his Milan newspaper office the next day. Grandson and namesake of the Italian monarch who helped unite Italy, Victor Emmanuel III invited Mussolini to become prime minister and form a working government.

The fasces symbol—sometimes shown without the ax head—is used in many places, including the United States. There is one in the statue of George Washington at Federal Hall in New York, another on the Mercury dime, and two on the front of Abraham Lincoln's chair at the Lincoln Memorial. There are also fasces displayed on the walls of the U.S. House of Representatives. [Wikimedia Commons]

Benito Mussolini arrived in Rome in the relative comfort of a sleeper car. He had considered getting off the overnight train early to symbolically complete the trip into Rome on horseback, but he decided against that strategy. Even for Mussolini, it was too over-the-top. Accompanied by bodyguards, he first stopped at a hotel and changed his clothes. Then Mussolini walked into the royal palace.

The king declared Mussolini "a man of purpose," and he became Italy's prime minister.

Crowds lined the streets as the Fascists marched out of Rome in a five-hour parade. The story of the March on Rome quickly acquired the weight of legend. The number of Blackshirt marchers has long been disputed but was probably no more than thirty thousand. In time, the Fascists claimed much larger numbers.

Every country has its history and its legends. Often the legends are created to form a proud, patriotic narrative of national identity and create a foundation story that unites the people. Sometimes, it is as simple as the story of George Washington chopping down the cherry tree, a story that has no basis in fact. Such legends can be powerful, but they are not the same as history.

In the case of Italy and Mussolini's march, the truth was quite different from the legend. Far from being a power-seizing coup, the march had been a calculated piece of political theater. In all, about a dozen people died around the country in this aborted and contrived armed rebellion. Fascist propaganda later exaggerated that death toll to the thousands to make the march seem more heroic.

Mussolini had used an entirely staged moment and an extravagant threat of rebellion to gain the reins of power. Eventually, a generation of Italian schoolchildren would be taught his "official" heroic version of valiant Fascist marchers rescuing Italy.

"The truth was more mundane," according to Harvard professors Steven Levitsky and Daniel Ziblatt. "The squads of Fascists around the country were a menace, but Mussolini's machinations to take the reins of state were no revolution." Victor Emmanuel III, they point out, saw Mussolini as "a rising political star and means of neutralizing unrest." Mussolini also had the support of conservative politicians and religious leaders, who feared the Socialists and Communists. "They saw Mussolini as someone they could hide behind, manipulate, and when convenient, replace," writes Madeleine Albright, the former U.S. secretary of state. "But Mussolini . . . had a talent for theater and little respect for the courage of his adversaries." In his first speech as prime minister, he boasted he could have turned the hall of parliament into a camp for his Blackshirts.

Some of the people who supported Mussolini made the misjudgment that they could rein him in. But for the next twenty-three years, his Fascists ruled Italy, establishing control of the government in one-party rule. Soon after Mussolini came to power, a liberal Italian politician coined a new word: **totalitarianism**, a government in which the state controls all political and economic matters. Mussolini liked the idea.

★

Mussolini and his Blackshirts march through Rome.
[Wikimedia Commons]

Who was this preening, posturing man who enthralled a nation?

Benito Amilcare Andrea Mussolini was born on July 29, 1883, in the small town of Predappio, the son of a poor black-smith named Alessandro Mussolini. His mother, Rosa, was a schoolteacher, and the family lived in two small rooms on the second floor of a dilapidated palazzo. While Rosa was a devout Catholic, Alessandro Mussolini wrote for Socialist journals and was frequently found arguing politics in local taverns. A dedicated Socialist, he named his firstborn son after Benito Juárez, the president of Mexico widely admired by Italian revolutionaries.

Even today, the word *socialist* is tossed around freely and often with great misunderstanding. First used in English around 1830, the term **socialism** in its most basic sense means a system in which property, natural resources, and the distribution of income are subject to social control. The idea of a society in which everything is shared equally is much older, going back to the ideas of Plato's *Republic* and early Christian communities in which labor and goods were shared by all members of the community. Under a pure form of socialism, in theory, everything that is produced is owned by the people and allocated by the government for the benefit of the people, according to their needs.

This system stands in stark contrast to **capitalism**, or free enterprise, in which individuals and organizations, not a central government, control a society's means of production. Under the capitalist economy, which had evolved gradually in Europe in the late Middle Ages and quickened in the sixteenth through eighteenth centuries, all prices, supplies, and distribution of products and services are determined—at least in theory—by free markets. This includes wages and other compensation paid to the workers who produce the goods.

In such a system, competition determines prices; investments are driven by the most efficient use of resources; and wealth and property are privately owned. The purest form of capitalism is free market or laissez-faire capitalism, in which governments do not restrict or regulate private individuals. Most modern countries, including the United States, practice a mixed capitalist system that includes a degree of regulation. In many of these countries, taxes pay for social services that may include a form of national health care and retirement income, such as Social Security in the United States.

Many of the basic ideals of capitalism were laid out in 1776 by Scottish philosopher Adam Smith in *The Wealth of Nations*, often called the bible of capitalism. Smith wrote, "Every man, as long as he does not violate the laws of justice, is left perfectly free to pursue his own interest in his own way, and to bring both his industry and capital into competition with those of any other man or order of men."

By the early twentieth century, socialism had emerged as the chief counterpoint to capitalism as the ideal economic system. It appealed to poor workers or those of modest means, including those who farmed for large landowners, who shared in little of the rewards of their labor. The idea of inequality had come down through the ages from ancient Greece and Rome, through the medieval system of serfdom, and still divided the haves and the have-nots.

Winning many followers from the working classes, the socialist idea became a major force in European politics. Socialism's spread was largely inspired by two influential works, *The Communist Manifesto* of 1848, written by Germans Karl Marx and Friedrich Engels, and *Das Kapital*, written by Marx, in three volumes published from 1867 to 1894.

"The history of all hitherto existing society is the history of class struggles," states *The Communist Manifesto*. "Freeman and slave, patrician and plebeian, lord and serf, guild-master and journeyman, in a word oppressor and oppressed, stood in constant opposition to one another, carried on an uninterrupted, now hidden, now open fight, a fight that each time ended, either in a revolutionary reconstitution of society at large, or in the common ruin of the contending classes."

Mussolini was profoundly influenced by his father's strong socialist beliefs. But his mother's Catholicism steered his education. He was sent to a strict Roman Catholic boarding school where he once stabbed a schoolmate with a penknife and was expelled for his offenses. Sent to another boarding school, Mussolini stabbed another fellow student, but this time he was only suspended and allowed to return the next term. Mussolini was intelligent and passed his exams, obtained a teaching diploma, and worked briefly as a schoolteacher.

Is there some clue in this wild, violent youth to suggest the despot to come? It seems unlikely. After all, if every boy who has ever been expelled from school for fighting—or even attacking someone with a penknife—became a dictator, the world would have far more dictators.

With little interest in teaching, Mussolini discovered his true passion in writing and politics. At the age of nineteen, he left Italy for Switzerland in 1902, carrying a medallion of Karl Marx. Like his father, who died in 1910, Mussolini had become a devoted Socialist, rejecting the Catholicism of his mother, who died in 1905. By then, Mussolini was also reading Friedrich Nietzsche, the German writer, philosopher, and prominent atheist who in 1882 famously proclaimed, "God is dead."

Mussolini was also drawn to Nietzsche's concept of a "Superman" (*Übermensch*). Nietzsche wrote, "I want to teach men the sense of their existence, which is the Superman." This Superman was not a costumed, faster-than-a-speeding-bullet superhero from a comic book or Hollywood blockbuster, but a superior individual who could cast off the constraints of religion (with promises of an afterlife) to find real meaning on earth.

Nietzsche died before Mussolini and Hitler gained power, but both Mussolini and Hitler appropriated some of his ideas as the underpinning of the nationalistic idea of "master races" that later drove the Fascists and Nazis.

Filled with notions of socialism and *Übermensch* philosophy, Mussolini acquired a reputation as a charismatic, mesmerizing speaker and a gifted writer. Swiss police were less impressed by his skills. The authorities in Bern once jailed him for twelve days after he called for a general strike at a May Day rally. They deported him, but Mussolini promptly boarded a train and traveled to Lausanne, Switzerland, where the Bern order did not apply. Eventually, Mussolini returned to Italy to fulfill the mandatory military service he had tried to evade. After his discharge, he returned to teaching but still continued his Socialist agitating. He was jailed and released several more times before becoming editor of a new Socialist paper, *La Lotta di Classe* (The Class Struggle). Later he was named editor of Italy's main Socialist journal, *Avanti!* (Forward).

In 1914, the war cries were growing louder across Europe. Like many Socialists, Mussolini rejected the war that was coming. Many poor and working-class people saw the conflict as a struggle among kings and national leaders who wanted to expand their empires. They knew that they would have to fight but had little to gain from the coming war, so the Italian socialists were advocating for Italy to remain neutral. But a few months after war broke out in August, Mussolini switched positions. He came to advocate intervention on the side of the Allies, persuaded that the defeat of France would be the deathblow to liberty in Europe. He resigned from *Avanti!* and started another paper, *Il Popolo d'Italia* (The People of Italy). The Socialists expelled him.

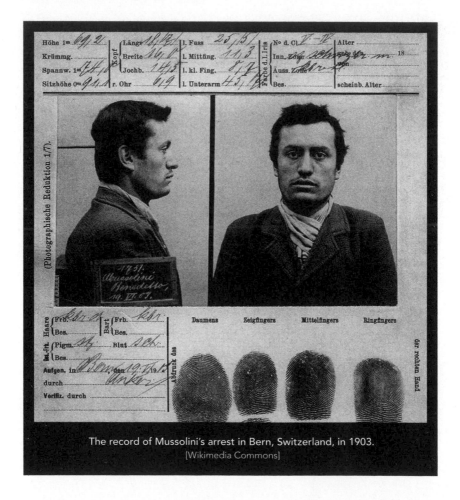

The record of Mussolini's arrest in Bern, Switzerland, in 1903.
[Wikimedia Commons]

To gain popular support, many nations tried to cast the war as a crusade for national greatness. The appeal to patriotism and nationalism took hold in several countries, including Italy. Mussolini argued that Italy must join the Great War to retake Italian territory in the Austro-Hungarian Empire, Germany's ally. Mussolini did not publicly reveal that his new opinions were partly fueled by the funds he secretly received from an Italian arms manufacturer who wanted to promote the war as good for business.

After Italy declared war in May 1915, Mussolini wrote in *Il Popolo*, "From today onward we are all Italians and nothing but Italians. Now that steel has met steel, one single cry comes from our hearts—*Viva l'Italia!* [Long live Italy!]"

He was drafted into the army and served on the front lines near the Isonzo River, which ran along the border of northern Italy and Austria. Wounded seriously by an accidental explosion in his trench during training exercises, Mussolini was hospitalized for months. While recovering, he was introduced to Italy's king Victor Emmanuel III, who was making an official visit to the wounded, an incident later given far more importance by Fascist propaganda. Discharged from the hospital in June 1917, he returned to his newspaper. That fall, after a devastating Italian defeat, British intelligence services started secretly paying Mussolini to tamp down growing antiwar sentiment in his country. Maintaining Italy as an ally would help the British in the fight against Germany and the Austro-Hungarian Empire.

When the war ended in November 1918, Mussolini's writing

Mussolini in uniform as a *bersagliere*, a sharpshooter of the Italian infantry, during World War I. [Wikimedia Commons]

had a new edge. Italy had lost more than half a million men to wartime death, and many more were wounded and left handicapped, losses that fell most heavily on the poor and working classes. The country had not been rewarded with new territory, as other victors were, and Italy was mockingly called an "honorary loser." Mussolini was calling for the emergence of a man "ruthless and energetic enough to make a clean sweep" to revive the Italian nation—a man who sounded very much like Nietzsche's Superman. Mussolini would later tell fellow Fascists that "only the intelligent and the strong-willed" had the right to decide the country's fate.

Before his rise to power, Italy's poverty, unemployment, crime, and corruption, along with a weak king and parliament incapable of governing, left the country nearly paralyzed. Like Weimar Germany, post–World War I Italy suffered from crippling social discontent, limited job opportunities, and growing fears of a Socialist uprising. Even though Italy had fought on the winning side in that war, many Italians felt cheated out of the spoils of war.

In March 1919, Mussolini and a group of fellow veterans created the political party Fasci di Combattimento, its name evoking the ancient Roman symbol, with about three hundred members. Violently anti-Socialist while still claiming to support poor and working-class Italians, the Fascists began to appeal to unemployed war veterans, who resented the growing Socialist movement, which called them dupes for serving in an unjust war. These former soldiers, including the elite Arditi, had organized themselves into roving squads, wearing black shirts and trousers and red fez caps. The armed squads of Blackshirts terrorized their political opponents all over Italy.

"Populists are antiestablishment politicians—figures who, claiming to represent the voice of 'the people,' wage war on what they depict as a corrupt and conspiratorial elite," write the political scientists Steven Levitsky and Daniel Ziblatt. "Populists tend to deny the legitimacy of established parties, attacking them as undemocratic and even unpatriotic. They tell voters that the existing system is not really a democracy but instead has been hijacked, corrupted, or rigged by the elite. And they promise to bury that elite and return power to 'the people.'"

These authors warn that populists who win elections often assault democracy and move toward authoritarianism. They list four warning signs of an authoritarian:

1. **Rejection of the democratic rules of the game**
2. **Denial of the legitimacy of political opponents**
3. **Toleration or encouragement of violence**

4. Readiness to curtail civil liberties of opponents, including media

Eventually Mussolini would be four for four.

Turning more ruthless, Mussolini began to employ textbook examples of an authoritarian's path to power. The Fascist Party "banned rival parties, arbitrarily imprisoned or drove into exile their leaders and, before and after 1922, killed from 2,000 to 3,000 of its political opponents," according to biographer R. J. B. Bosworth. "It destroyed the free press, liquidated non-Fascist trade unions, infringed the rule of law, sponsored a secret police, [and] tempted Italians to spy on, and inform against, each other."

After the March on Rome, Prime Minister Mussolini ramped up his violence for political advantage. Voter intimidation and fraud gave the Fascists a clear majority in parliament in the 1924 election. After the election, a prominent Socialist politician named Giacomo Matteotti was abducted and stuffed into a waiting car. Several days before his kidnapping, Matteotti had passionately denounced the fraud and violence committed by the Fascists. He was trying to have the legislature declare the elections invalid. Two months later, his decomposed body was discovered.

Despite evidence that Matteotti had been killed by a Fascist hit squad, the king did nothing. The most powerful members of Italy's elite—prominent politicians, businessmen, and Vatican priests—also went along, still hoping that Mussolini would provide a strong government and hold back what these elites viewed as the growing threat of Socialism.

The Fascist violence against political opponents, and sometimes even priests, and success in winning the masses concealed what the Fascists represented. In Mussolini's words, Fascism meant a system in which "all is for the state, nothing is outside the state, nothing and no one are against the state." This was a confusing smokescreen of gibberish.

On Christmas Eve in 1925, Mussolini—who began calling himself Il Duce (The Leader)—was given the title *capo del governo* (head of government). By 1926, Il Duce had consolidated power for himself, transforming Italy into a single-party state. "I, and I alone, am responsible," he claimed. Laws were drafted and quickly passed by the legislature, now dominated by Fascists. The courts were also increasingly packed with friendly judges willing to do Mussolini's bidding.

No small part of Mussolini's hold on the country came from propaganda, as the Fascists took total control of the press and enlarged the cult of personality around Mussolini. A cult of personality arises when a regime uses the techniques of mass media, propaganda, buildings or roads with the person's name or image, intense patriotism, and government-organized demonstrations or rallies to create a heroic or even godlike image of a leader. Using excessive flattery and praise, the cult of personality is what might be called "celebrity on steroids."

Mussolini did all these things. His image was everywhere as loyal newspapers and magazines ran heroic photographs of him, all reviewed by Mussolini before publication. Fascist editors were placed in control of major Italian newspapers. Opposition newspapers were shut down or forced into hiding, with editors and writers beaten by Fascist thugs. Journalists were required to join an order of writers controlled by the Fascists.

Mussolini also quickly grasped the importance of movies, which at the time were just beginning to emerge as mass entertainment. The Fascist-controlled government eventually required that theaters show Fascist-supplied news clips. Italians flocking to movies soon saw an endless series of newsreels in which Mussolini dedicated new projects, laid wreaths at the graves of war heroes and Fascist martyrs, rode on horseback in an open-necked shirt, or inspected works projects in a dashing white suit. This was the cult of personality in action, and Mussolini became the face of Fascism. One party leader said, "Fascism is not a party but a religion; it is the future of the country."

The Fascists' control extended to the Italian universities, including some of the oldest universities in the world. In 1931, they demanded that professors swear an oath of allegiance, pledging "fidelity to the King, to his Royal successors and to the Fascist regime." Only twelve of some twelve hundred university professors refused to take the oath. They lost their positions. One of the Strongman's essential techniques is to control education and eliminate free thought in order to quell any form of opposition to his ideas and policies. Pressure and violence aimed at intellectuals, artists, and writers are central to that strategy.

Even the Italian calendar became Fascist propaganda. In addition to the anniversary of the March on Rome, Mussolini established a new national holiday to commemorate the founding of the Roman Empire. He also abolished celebrations marking the day Rome became part of Italy and those marking the workers' holiday, May Day, which was declared foreign and Socialist. Likening itself to the French revolutionaries of the eighteenth century, the party also began dating history from the March on Rome, adding Roman numerals after the traditional date to indicate the Fascist year.

Mussolini was applauded by many politicians outside Italy, including Winston Churchill, later famed as Great Britain's wartime prime minister, the leader of the crusade against Hitler. World leaders welcomed Mussolini as a counterforce to the threat of Communism following the Russian Revolution led by Vladimir Lenin and his Bolsheviks in 1917. After a visit to Rome in 1927, Churchill spoke admiringly of Mussolini, although his opinion later changed when Mussolini joined forces with Hitler.

Mussolini's popularity was also driven by the appearance that Italy was a nation on the move.

Under Mussolini, the military rearmed, and Italy soon had a powerful Mediterranean navy. Massive public works programs aimed at creating jobs for the unemployed included razing sections of Rome to uncover the city's ancient ruins. One of those excavations in the 1920s uncovered four temples and part of the Theater of Pompey, where the Roman Senate was meeting when Caesar was assassinated.

Another of the most enduring symbols of Mussolini's Fascist rule is Milan's central train station. Completed in 1931, the

Built as a monument to Fascism in 1931, the central train station in Milan features symbols of ancient Rome, including the fasces used throughout the design. [Wikimedia Commons]

building was decorated at Mussolini's insistence with elaborate sculptures of mythical beasts like winged horses and displays of the Roman SPQR symbol. The building also featured the fasces, the ancient Roman symbol of strength and authority used as the emblem of the Fascist Party.

But Mussolini's Italy could boast of some real accomplishments. Italian inventors and industrialists developed the world's fastest propeller seaplane and the passenger ship *Rex*, which held the speed record for a westbound transatlantic crossing between 1933 and 1935. Italian products such as Fiat automobiles and Olivetti typewriters were marketed around the world, setting the standard for modern design.

At the time, the most prominent Italian in the world was Guglielmo Marconi, pioneer of radio communications and the winner of the Nobel Prize in Physics in 1909. After the fighting in World War I ended, Marconi went to the 1919 Versailles peace talks as a member of the Italian delegation. According to Marc Raboy, author of *Marconi: The Man Who Networked the World*, the renowned inventor sought U.S. president Woodrow Wilson's support of Italian claims to parts of the defeated Austro-Hungarian Empire. After Italy's claims were ignored, Marconi threw his support behind Mussolini. Hoping that the Fascists would restore Italy's grandeur, Marconi joined the party in 1923. Recent research suggests that as early as 1930, Marconi kept Jewish scientists from joining the Academy of Italy, which Mussolini had created "to further the genius of our race, and to favor its expansion abroad."

Mussolini also understood the value of sports, both in everyday life and as propaganda. In 1933, he cheered as Italian boxer Primo Carnera became the world heavyweight champion in a time when that title was far more significant than it is today.

An Olivetti typewriter.
[Wikimedia Commons]

The following year, Italy hosted the World Cup, the championship of international soccer. Under the Fascists, soccer had been aggressively promoted as a means of building Italian pride. A national league, known as Serie A, had been created to improve Italy's standing as the sport gained international prominence in the postwar world. "The intent was twofold," writes Simon Martin, a historian of Italian sport. "Firstly, to forge a sense of national identity and, secondly, to create a stronger, more competitive structure that would result in a national team capable of rivalling the best. . . . The generation bloomed in 1934 as Italy hosted and won the World Cup."

Mussolini clearly intended the World Cup as propaganda showcasing the accomplishments of Italy under his regime. Mussolini got what he wanted—a world stage and a victory. In

Guglielmo Marconi, winner of the Nobel Prize in Physics for his role in developing the radio, was an international celebrity who later became a Mussolini loyalist. [Wikimedia Commons]

1938, Italy repeated as champions. Mussolini welcomed the winning team to Rome, just as U.S. presidents bring champions of different sports to the White House in a show of pride and patriotism.

In addition to Italy's success in creating a new image of a muscular, modern nation, Mussolini understood another key source of power to control the future: a new generation of Italian children loyal to Mussolini and the party. The Fascists created an array of clubs and service organizations for Italian children. Focused on physical fitness and paramilitary training for boys, the Fascist youth clubs started at age six and went to twenty-one. Eight- to fourteen-year-old boys were enrolled in the Balilla, the most prominent and largest of the youth clubs. Though modeled on the Boy Scout movement begun by British general Robert Baden-Powell, the Balilla became much more militant under the leadership of a former Arditi soldier, Renato Ricci. The last of their Ten Commandments was *"Il Duce ha sempre ragione"* (Il Duce is always right).

Besides letting impressionable young boys play at being soldiers, these youth organizations had a grander purpose— indoctrinating an entire population loyal to Fascism. "The totalitarian state had, after all, created a network of youth organizations in which all Italians of the so-called 'generation of Mussolini' were meant to muster," writes biographer Bosworth. The youngest children, ages six to seven, belonged to the Figli della Lupa (Children of the Wolf), a name recalling Rome's legendary beginnings. Groups for girls, such as the Piccole italiane (Little Italian Girls) for ages eight to thirteen, promoted the ideals of domesticity and motherhood. Boys fourteen to seventeen were enrolled in the Avanguardisti (Vanguards). Young men and women between eighteen and twenty-one belonged, respectively, to the Giovani fascisti and the Giovani fasciste (Young Fascists).

In every gym and camp, there were guns for the children to carry. Newsreels showed squads of uniformed Italian children marching in line. "One treasured ceremony, repeated in many town *piazze* across the peninsula, had a Giovane Fascista passing a rifle to an Avanguardista and then to a Balilla and even a Figlio della Lupa, with the strident message that they were handing on the torch of militant life," writes Bosworth.

Young Italian boys in the Fascist Youth Organization called Balilla, part of a nationwide program to win the loyalty of Italian children under Fascist rule. The *M* on their uniform is for Mussolini. [Wikimedia Commons]

And war was one of Mussolini's key routes to establishing a new Italian empire. Having gained little from the Versailles Treaty, he wanted to expand Italy's few colonial possessions in northern Africa.

In 1935, he dispatched a hundred thousand troops armed with modern weapons to Ethiopia (then called Abyssinia) to establish control over a new colony. "The contest was hopelessly unequal: machine guns, bombers, and mustard gas against half-naked tribesmen armed with bolt-action rifles," historian Robert Hughes writes. "They overran Abyssinia, and even emphasized their complete victory with such propaganda gestures as building, with army labor, a colossal stone-concrete-and-earth portrait of mighty Mussolini as a sphinx, rising from the sand." Ethiopia was incorporated into the new Italian empire.

Between 1936 and 1939, Mussolini also sent more than seventy thousand Italian soldiers to fight alongside the forces of right-wing leader General Francisco Franco in Spain's civil war. Franco opposed the democratic republic established in Spain in 1931 and launched a coup to take over the country, leading to a civil war that claimed as many as five hundred thousand lives. Both Mussolini and another Strongman, Adolf Hitler of Germany, supported Franco.

Mussolini's ambitions had found a powerful new partner in Hitler. Watching the developments in Germany under the Nazis, Mussolini ordered the Italian press to take a pro-German line. A new relationship between kindred spirits emerged when the two Strongmen informally agreed to a Rome-Berlin Axis in October 1936.

In May 1938, Hitler visited Rome, and Mussolini made sure he was welcomed to the Italian capital as a conquering hero. As Mussolini came under the growing influence of Hitler, Il Duce copied the Nazi Party's Nuremberg Laws, stripping Italian Jews of their civil rights in 1938. On May 22, 1939, Germany and Italy formalized their alliance with the Pact of Steel.

Mussolini and Hitler in 1936 after the declaration of the Rome-Berlin Axis.
[Wikimedia Commons]

World War II was only months away.

Benito Mussolini is not usually counted among the worst of the Strongmen who altered the course of world history in the first half of the twentieth century. But he was a ruthless dictator who set the stage for what was to follow. Mussolini came first and helped inspire Hitler. In time, he would fall under Hitler's shadow. Charlie Chaplin's 1940 satire *The Great Dictator* used the figure of Benzino Napaloni to mock Mussolini as the comical sidekick to Adenoid Hynkel, the Chaplin character modeled on Hitler.

But there was nothing funny about Hitler and Mussolini. As Hitler gained power in Europe, Mussolini increasingly seemed a lesser figure. But Mussolini's daring March on Rome had paved the way for the German führer. Mussolini used violence and murder to stamp out opposition. Hitler watched what Mussolini had accomplished in bringing a nation to heel and employed similar techniques in Germany.

Although he preceded Hitler and provided some inspiration, Mussolini eventually came to be seen as one of Hitler's willing accomplices. And he must be held accountable for his role in Hitler's crimes against humanity. While the direct death toll from Mussolini's actions is far smaller than that of Hitler, Mussolini had employed banned chemical weapons in Libya and Ethiopia and later sent thousands of Italian Jews to their deaths in Nazi camps.

Primo Levi, a young chemist and "Italian citizen of Jewish race," was captured by Fascists in December 1943 and sent to a detention camp in northern Italy. From there, he and other

In 1940, the silent film star Charlie Chaplin made a satirical film about Hitler called *The Great Dictator*. It included a character named Benzino Napaloni, a parody of Italy's Benito Mussolini, played by actor Jack Oakie who was nominated for a Best Supporting Actor Academy Award.
[Wikimedia Commons]

Italian Jews were sent to Auschwitz, the Nazi concentration camp in Poland. Many already knew what the journey meant. Levi survived Auschwitz and later wrote of the night before leaving Italy:

All took leave from life in the manner which most suited them. Some praying, some deliberately drunk, others lustfully intoxicated for the last time. But the mothers stayed up to prepare the food for the journey with tender care, and washed their children and packed the luggage; and at dawn, the barbed wire was full of children's washing hung out in the wind to dry. Nor did they forget the diapers, the toys, the cushions and the hundred other small things which mothers remember and which children always need. Would you not do the same? If you and your child were going to be killed tomorrow, would you not give him to eat today?

Mussolini's alliance with Germany—later to include Japan as well—eventually brought the Second World War to Italy. Allied bombings of Italian cities and an invasion of Sicily in July 1943 ended Mussolini's reign. His outsized ambition was his undoing.

Mussolini and Hitler ride together in Munich, Germany, in 1938.
[Wikimedia Commons]

As the Allies made headway in Sicily, Mussolini was deposed by his own Fascist ministers and placed under arrest. The new government in Rome opened secret peace negotiations with the Allies, and Italy formally surrendered in September 1943, joining the Allies for the rest of the war. Hitler ordered German forces to occupy the country and sent commandos to rescue Mussolini, who was briefly installed as the dictator of a German puppet state in northern Italy.

As the Allied forces advanced north through Italy in April 1945, Mussolini tried to escape into Switzerland with a German convoy. Italian partisans who had been fighting the Fascists as well as the Nazis searched the convoy and captured Mussolini and his entourage. Although there are differing accounts of Mussolini's final days, he was executed by the partisans on April 28, 1945, along with his mistress and other Fascist leaders. Their bodies were dumped in front of a half-built garage on Milan's main town square, where their corpses were stoned, pelted by vegetables, kicked, and spat on. Then the bodies were strung up by the ankles so that they could be seen above the large crowd that had gathered. Later buried in an unmarked grave, Mussolini's corpse was eventually recovered by Fascist admirers and hidden for years. In 1957, his body was reinterred in Predappio in a tomb now decorated with Fascist images. Visitors still come to the town to honor Mussolini, especially on the anniversary of his death.

Benito Mussolini was a Strongman—a dictator who used any means he could to acquire power. He proved himself ruthless, violent, and uncompromising. Like all other Strongmen,

Mussolini on April 25, 1945, the last known photograph of him alive.
[Wikimedia Commons]

Mussolini did not kill opponents, rule a nation, and help bring the world to war by himself. At every step in his ascent, he had the full support of accomplices, some even more murderous than Mussolini himself. He also won the support of other politicians and businessmen and religious leaders, who all thought that they could control Mussolini once he was given power—a fatal error that has been repeated throughout history. Once in control of the government, Mussolini understood that power brings more power. But as the English historian Lord Acton famously said well before Mussolini came to power, "Power tends to corrupt and absolute power corrupts absolutely. Great men are almost always bad men."

THE LIFE OF ADOLF HITLER

April 20, 1889 ··· Hitler is born in Braunau am Inn, a village in Austria.

1915-1918 ··· Hitler serves in World War I.

Aug. 11, 1919 ··· Germany adopts a new constitution in the town of Weimar, giving the democratic government its unofficial name of Weimar Republic.

1920 ··· The German Workers' Party adds *National Socialist* to its name, becoming the Nazi Party.

Nov. 8-9, 1923 ··· Hitler attempts to overthrow the government in the Beer Hall Putsch.

Feb. 26, 1924 ··· Hitler is tried for treason and sentenced to five years in prison.

1925 ··· *Mein Kampf*, written by Hitler in prison, is published.

Nov. 6, 1932 ··· Nazi Party wins 34 percent of the seats in parliament.

Jan. 30, 1933 ··· President Hindenburg appoints Hitler chancellor of Germany.

Feb. 28, 1933 ··· Reichstag Fire Decree suspends constitutional rights to personal liberty, freedom of expression, and right to assemble.

March 22, 1933 ··· Dachau concentration camp opens.

March 23, 1933 ··· The Enabling Act gives Hitler power to make laws independent of the parliament.

July 14, 1933 ··· The German parliament makes the Nazi Party the only legal party.

June 30, 1934 ··· Night of the Long Knives: Nazi storm troopers are executed in a wave of killings as Hitler consolidates his power.

Aug. **1934**	Hitler becomes führer of Germany.
Sept. 15, **1935**	Hitler announces Nuremberg Laws, which define German citizenship by blood and ban marriage between Jews and Germans.
Aug. **1936**	Hitler presides over the Berlin Olympics.
March **1938**	*The Anschluss*: Germany annexes Austria.
Sept. **1938**	Munich Agreement permits Hitler to take control of part of Czechoslovakia in hopes of avoiding a war.
Nov. 9, **1938**	Kristallnacht: Jewish shops and synagogues are raided and destroyed.
Sept. 1, **1939**	Germany invades Poland, triggering World War II.
June 22, **1941**	Operation Barbarossa: Germany invades Soviet Union.
Jan. **1942**	Nazi leaders discuss "Final Solution" to exterminate the Jewish population.
July 17, **1942**-Feb. 2, **1943**	The Battle of Stalingrad is fought.
June 6, **1944**	D-Day: Allies land in Normandy, France.
Spring **1945**	The Allies and Soviets advance on Berlin.
April 30, **1945**	Hitler commits suicide in Berlin.

CHAPTER

★ ★ ★ **4** ★ ★ ★

THE BIG LIE

The Olympic flame enters Olympic Stadium in August 1936. The 1936 Olympics introduced the torch relay, which is now a tradition. [Wikimedia Commons]

THE STORY

OF

ADOLF HITLER

The great masses of the people . . . more easily fall
victim to a big lie than to a little one.

—**Adolf Hitler,** *Mein Kampf*

• • •

After fifteen years of work I have achieved, as a common
German soldier and merely with my fanatical will power,
the unity of the German nation, and have freed it from
the death sentence of Versailles.

—**Adolf Hitler**

• • •

We will not be silent. We are your bad conscience.
The White Rose will not leave you in peace!

—**White Rose resistance leaflet**

• • •

The present destruction of Europe would not be as
complete and thorough had the German people not
accepted freely its plan, participated voluntarily in its
execution, and up to this point profited greatly therefrom.

—**Raphael Lemkin,** *Axis Rule in Occupied Europe*

• • •

BERLIN, GERMANY

AUGUST 1936

ALL EYES WERE ON Berlin. It was 1936 and Adolf Hitler wanted to charm the world. With the Olympics taking place in Germany, Hitler planned to dazzle visitors with an international coming-out party. He would trumpet the majesty of his revived nation's new architectural wonders. He would showcase a proud Germany, rising out of the ashes of its humbling defeat in the Great War. And he would put his country's superior athletes on display.

In a newly built, swastika-draped stadium, they would prove that what he had been defiantly declaring was true: Germany was the home of an "Aryan" master race, which was purported to be superior to "Semites," "yellows," and "blacks." Members of this so-called race were credited with all the progress that benefited humanity The German "Aryan" race was gifted with this biological superiority, Hitler asserted, to rule a vast empire across Eastern Europe.

Many Germans agreed. With one approving voice, the massed spectators in Berlin roared *"Heil Hitler"* as they raised the stiff-armed Nazi salute when the games opened.

But a remarkable young African American man named Jesse Owens had other plans. A strong German team was expected to excel in the track and field events. But against the backdrop of red-and-black Nazi banners swirling around the hundred-thousand-seat stadium, Jesse Owens dominated every time he walked onto the track.

"When Owens finished competing, the African-American son of a sharecropper and the grandson of slaves had single-handedly crushed Hitler's myth of Aryan supremacy," sports columnist Larry Schwartz writes. "He gave four virtuoso performances, winning gold medals in the 100- and 200-meter dashes, the long jump and on America's 4x100 relay team. Score it: Owens 4, Hitler 0."

Thousands of Germans give the Nazi salute at the opening of the Berlin Olympic Games. [Wikimedia Commons]

Jesse Owens competes in the Berlin Olympics. [Wikimedia Commons]

What Jesse Owens had done was remarkable. But his cele-brated victories did not change the arc of history. The Olympics still proved to be a propaganda boon for the Nazis. Despite Owens's golden performance, Germany still won eighty-nine medals, the most of any country. That included thirty-three gold medals. "Hitler's Germany was open to viewing for visitors from all over the world," Hitler biographer Ian Kershaw writes. "Most of them went away mightily impressed."

Many of the people who came to Berlin for the games came away dazzled at the cleanliness and order they had seen in Germany. A *New York Times* correspondent described the Berlin games as the "biggest and showiest athletic contest ever staged," and the head of the U.S. Olympic Committee marveled at the dedication of the German athletes he had seen. But many foreign visitors to Berlin didn't know that "undesirables" had been swept from the streets and placed in camps. Nor could they know that the next two scheduled Olympic Games would be scrapped. World War II meant the cancellation of the Olympics in 1940 and 1944.

When the Berlin Olympics opened in 1936, it had been a little more than three years since Hitler was appointed chancellor and used the Reichstag Fire Decree to tighten his grip on Germany. In almost no time, he had secured unlimited power for himself and the Nazis, having hundreds of his political rivals assassinated. He had abolished the office of president after President Hindenburg's death, declared himself führer (leader), and placed every level of government in complete Nazi control. "The personality cult built around Hitler had reached new levels of idolatry and made millions of new converts as the 'people's chancellor,'" writes Kershaw.

How had this otherwise unremarkable survivor of the First World War come to mesmerize a nation, seize power so quickly, and, at least for a time, impress many observers around the world as a forceful leader who had put on such a dazzling show in Berlin?

Adolf Hitler was born to Alois and Klara Hitler in one of the upper-floor apartments of a three-story house on Salzburger Vorstadt in Braunau am Inn, Austria—then part of the Austro-Hungarian Empire—on April 20, 1889. He lived there until the age of three.

Hitler's father, Alois, had been born illegitimately in 1837 to a farmer's daughter named Maria Schicklgruber. The identity of

Adolf Hitler (seated, far right) with other men in the Sixteenth Bavarian Reserve Infantry Regiment during World War I. [Wikimedia Commons]

Alois Shicklgruber's father is unknown. There has been speculation that Hitler's grandfather was Jewish, but no evidence has been found to support the notion. When Alois was five, his mother married a poor local man, and a series of name changes followed. Records later showed that in 1876 Alois took the last name Hitler, and he was officially recognized as the legitimate son of Georg Hitler.

"It is impossible to imagine Hitler's rise to power had he retained his father's original surname of Schicklgruber," Paul Ham writes of Hitler's parentage. "The image of hundreds of thousands of Germans raising their right arms and shouting *'Heil Schicklgruber!'* is not only laughable, it is impossible. Such is the power of a name."

Unlike Mussolini, Hitler did not grow up in poverty. His father was an Austrian customs official of modest means. Overbearing and strong-willed, Alois Hitler was "pompous, status-proud, strict, humourless, frugal, pedantically punctual, and devoted to duty," according to Kershaw. His mother, Klara, had met Alois while she worked as a housemaid; he was a widower with two children, and she became his third wife. Klara and Alois had three more children, but all of them died before Adolf was born, and so Klara Hitler was devoted to her surviving son's well-being. Hitler's parents later had another son—Edmund, who died of measles at age six—and a daughter named Paula. Hitler would recall that he was his "mother's darling."

"If he didn't have his way he got very angry," remembered Hitler's half brother, Alois Jr. "He took to no one and could be very heartless. He could fly into a rage over any triviality."

His strict father, over fifty years old when Hitler was born, was a demanding taskmaster. Alois beat his adolescent son, though that was certainly not unusual at the time. If childhood beatings made dictators, there would be many more murderous despots in the world.

From childhood on, Hitler always loved the popular novels of Karl May, an enormously successful German writer who spun fanciful, romantic adventure tales of the American West featuring a noble Apache warrior chief named Winnetou and his

German sidekick, Old Shatterhand. As his peers outgrew the novels, Hitler would recruit younger boys to play war games based on May's imagined tales of the Old West.

In school, Adolf was rebellious and something of a bully. Struggling with academics, Hitler showed interest only in drawing and dreamed of becoming an artist, despite mediocre grades in art class. His skeptical father thought the idea was ludicrous and insisted the boy prepare to become a respectable civil servant. Their arguments over his artistic ambitions led to more thrashings and abuse that sent Hitler into tantrums, which continued with intensity when Hitler became an adult.

After his father's death in 1903, Hitler was expelled from school for his poor performance. Sent to another school, he failed German and mathematics. By that point, still dreaming of an artist's life, Adolf Hitler basically dropped out of school. He told his mother he had lost his final report card, but a school director later discovered it. Hitler had used it as toilet paper.

With no prospects, the teenage Hitler went through a period of "parasitic idleness," as biographer Ian Kershaw describes Hitler's years of living at home painting, reading, and dreaming of being a great artist, all the while being looked after by his doting mother. Confirmed as a Catholic in 1904, he later abandoned all sense of religion. "At thirteen, fourteen, fifteen, I no longer believed in anything," he later said. "Certainly none of my friends believed in the so-called communion."

Hitler's dream was crushed when he was rejected by Vienna's Academy of Fine Arts in 1907. But after his mother's death at the end of the year, he moved to the capital anyway, without any clear plan. By 1909, the future führer was a twenty-year-old failed artist lining up for a bed in a shelter. Broke, homeless, and reduced to begging, Hitler eventually made a little money with a friend who hawked Hitler's watercolor postcards of Vienna to tourists.

While in Vienna, Hitler was introduced to two key political influences. The first was German racist nationalism, which made the "German master race" argument that Hitler later adopted. The second was the vocal anti-Semitism of Vienna mayor Karl Lueger, who cast Jews as enemies of the German middle and lower classes. "Greater Vienna must not turn into Greater Jerusalem!" Lueger declared. According to biographer Paul Ham, Lueger was "fighting to defend Christianity against 'a new Palestine' and regularly invoked the old Catholic hatred of these 'Christ-killers'"—a hateful term for Jewish people used by many Christians for centuries based on the incorrect idea that Jews were responsible for the death of Jesus, who was in fact crucified by Romans.

Coming into his share of an inheritance from his father at age twenty-four, Hitler moved to the German city of Munich in 1913, hoping to escape the Austrian military draft. The authorities caught up with him early in 1914, and Hitler pleaded poverty. Declaring him "unsuitable for military service," the draft board said he was "too weak, incapable of firing weapons"—a record he later sought to conceal.

But with the outbreak of war in August 1914, Hitler volunteered for action in the German army and was assigned to the Bavarian infantry. War fever was in the air with Germany's

"All-High Warlord," Kaiser Wilhelm II, promising his soldiers, "You will be home before the leaves have fallen from the trees."

Another young German who eagerly enlisted later described the mood. "We had bonded together into one large and enthusiastic group," German veteran Ernst Jünger wrote in a memoir. "We were enraptured by war. We had set out in a rain of flowers, in a drunken atmosphere of blood and roses. Surely the war had to supply us with what we wanted; the great, the overwhelming, the hallowed experience. We thought of it as manly, as action, a merry duelling party on flowered, blood-bedewed meadows."

There would be no "merry duelling party." Four long years of murderous combat in the muddy trenches followed. Facing off across those stark battle lines were soldiers who were often no more than boys from farms and factory floors. In its final year, the losses in the Great War were compounded by the plague of Spanish influenza, the 1918 pandemic that took the lives of millions of people around the world, including some four hundred thousand Germans.

But for Hitler, the war was what Ernst Jünger called a "hallowed experience." With only ten days of training and military drills, Hitler and his regiment were sent to France, where he was assigned as a runner, or courier, one of the most dangerous jobs on the Western Front. A runner carried orders on foot or by bicycle from headquarters to the commanders in the trenches. Like other runners, Hitler was exposed to enemy fire as his unit took part in some of the fiercest combat on the Western Front. Once a shell struck a command post minutes after Hitler left, killing many of the staff there. In October 1916, he was wounded in the left thigh when a shell exploded in the dispatch runner's dugout, and he spent two months in a Red Cross hospital in Germany.

Hitler was promoted to corporal, his highest rank in the war, and received the Iron Cross, First Class, a medal awarded for bravery in battle, in August 1918. In October 1918, as German losses mounted and the war neared its end, he fell victim to a gas attack. Retreating with his comrades from the British mustard gas, Hitler was temporarily blinded and clung to fellow soldiers as they were led by a comrade who was less affected. He was lying in a military hospital when word of Germany's surrender reached the wards on November 12, 1918. Hitler called this the "greatest villainy of the century."

Just as the war changed Mussolini, going to battle marked a turning point in Hitler's life. "The First World War made Hitler possible," writes biographer Ian Kershaw. "Without the experience of war, the humiliation of defeat, and the upheaval of revolution the failed artist and social drop-out would not have discovered what to do with his life by entering politics. . . . And without the trauma of war, defeat, and revolution . . . the demagogue would have been without an audience for his hate-filled message."

Like many Germans in the postwar period, Hitler was outraged by the terms Germany was forced to accept under the Treaty of Versailles, announced in June 1919. The new German government, the Weimar Republic, was obligated to pay $33 billion in war reparations—an enormous amount of money at the time—forcing Germany deep into debt. Germany also had to surrender its overseas colonies and give up territory to France and Poland.

Resentful and angry at the bitter pill forced on Germany, Hitler seethed. In September 1919, thirty-year-old Hitler attended a meeting of the German Workers' Party, a nationalist, anti-Semitic group. Initially he had gone to the meeting as an informant, assigned by the army to monitor the group. But he got into a heated discussion with a guest, and the party chairman was so impressed with Hitler's impassioned speech that he invited Hitler to return.

By then Hitler's own ideas about the defeat of Germany in the recent war, the danger of Socialism, and the role of Jews were taking clearer shape. He had had the chance to develop them during his deployment the month before as an "educational officer," reeducating troops who had been "infected" with Bolshevism.

"He immediately found he could strike a chord with his audience, that the way he spoke roused soldiers listening to him from their passivity and cynicism," writes Kershaw. "Hitler was in his element. For the first time in his life, he found something at which he was an unqualified success. Almost by chance, he stumbled across his greatest talent. As he himself put it, he could 'speak.'"

The party put him to work spreading his anger in Munich's beer halls, and he quickly made a name for himself as the party's most popular draw. He was spoken of as Germany's Mussolini. The party renamed itself the National Socialist

German Workers' Party (the official name of the Nazi Party), and in July 1921 Hitler became its leader.

Large crowds came to hear this curious, defiant army corporal who called for a radical, new German order and preached a vision of a revived Germany that would replace the impotent, inefficient democracy in power. In Hitler's vision, German greatness would be restored if democracy was abolished, all citizens unselfishly served the state, and individual rights were surrendered to the good of the nation. Claiming the superiority of the German race, Hitler blamed the nation's weakness on the Germans responsible for the surrender, the "November criminals," whom he described as "backstabbers." He also blasted Communists, who he claimed were trying to take over the country.

But it was not Hitler's words or ideas that dazzled listeners. It was his style. His nearly hypnotic performances—practiced and perfected before a mirror—left his audience enthralled and eager to join the party. Hitler led these throngs like a master conductor shaping an orchestra to his will. His words rose and fell like waves crashing on the shore. He captivated people with the power of a mythical Siren, making them want to belong to his crusade. And always, he came back to his rousing claims of German racial superiority. "Germany for Germans!" he implored the crowds, telling them that they were a "master race" that had been cheated out of their rightful place.

While his list of enemies was long, Hitler increasingly reserved his most poisonous rhetoric for the small minority of Jews, about 1 percent of the German population.

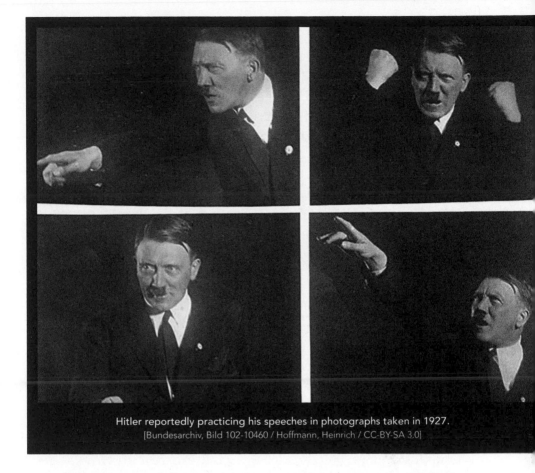

Hitler reportedly practicing his speeches in photographs taken in 1927.
[Bundesarchiv, Bild 102-10460 / Hoffmann, Heinrich / CC-BY-SA 3.0]

"Here was a messiah-like figure, willing to banish the Jews from the Lutheran temple," explains biographer Paul Ham. "To a country on its knees, this strangely charismatic speaker offered words that seemed to validate the nation's sacrifice and war record when nobody else would. . . . It was a measure of the depths of German despair, rather than any of Hitler's inherent qualities, that he managed to persuade so many."

Like Italy, postwar Germany was in economic crisis, and Hitler used the circumstances to his advantage. It was during this time that German people needed wheelbarrows to carry enough paper money to buy a loaf of bread. Goading discontented Germans, he quickly added some fifty-six thousand members to Nazi Party rolls, largely by blaming the nation's ills on the Jews.

As he organized the Nazi Party and added to its numbers, Hitler made clear that his goal was to rid Europe of Jews and other "inferior" peoples and absorb pure-blooded Aryans into a greatly expanded Germany—a Third Reich. The German word *Reich* means "realm" or "empire." The first two Reichs were the Holy Roman Empire of 800–1806 and the German Empire of 1871–1918. Hitler's plan called for an unrelenting war against the Slavic "hordes" of Russia and Eastern Europe, considered by Hitler to be *Untermenschen* (subhumans).

It is important to understand Hitler did not invent anti-Semitism. He was playing a new version of a very old theme. It was the toxic remnant of centuries of baseless hatred aimed at Jews that dated to ancient history and grew worse during medieval times in Christian Europe, continuing to modern times. In Russia, violent attacks against Jews, or pogroms, went back to the early nineteenth century. *Pogrom* comes from the Russian word for "devastation, destruction."

A pamphlet later known as *The Protocols of the Elders of Zion* first appeared in czarist Russia in 1903. Now known to be a completely fabricated piece of propaganda, it was written to blame Jews for a variety of social ills. According to the U.S. Holocaust Memorial Museum, "*Protocols* 'describes' the 'secret plans' of Jews to rule the world by manipulating the economy, controlling the media, and fostering religious conflict."

Although long discredited, it continues to circulate today with the single purpose of spreading hatred against Jewish people.

In 1920, the newspaper of prominent American industrialist and carmaker Henry Ford, the *Dearborn Independent*, began publishing material based on the *Protocols*. The articles, distributed in Ford dealerships throughout the country, accused the Jews of using Communism, banking, unions, and even entertainment like gambling and jazz to weaken the morals of American people.

By 1921, the Nazi Party had a newspaper and an official flag—which Hitler took credit for designing—featuring a hooked cross, or swastika. The hooked cross is an ancient symbol that is sacred in numerous religions, including Hinduism and Buddhism. In the nineteenth century, German archaeologist Heinrich Schliemann found swastikas at the site of ancient Troy and linked them to similar shapes on pottery in Germany. He speculated that the swastika was a "significant religious symbol of our remote ancestors."

Shortly after taking power in 1933, Hitler's regime replaced the Weimar Republic's tricolor flag of black, red, and gold with the black, white, and red of the old German Empire flag, which was flown alongside the Nazis' swastika. The swastika was soon found everywhere: on armbands, children's uniforms, and banners hanging from homes. In 1935, the Nazi flag became the official flag of the Third Reich, as part of its now notorious Nuremberg Laws, which deprived Jews of their German citizenship and denied them the right to marry Germans.

The Nazis also created a private army—the storm troopers,

or SA (from *Sturmabteilung*, meaning "assault division") — made up largely of unemployed and disenchanted World War I veterans. Known as the Brownshirts because of their uniform, they were led by veteran Ernst Röhm. Much like Mussolini's former Arditi soldiers, this force became Hitler's shock troops, with access to hidden stores of weapons and capable of terrible violence. By 1923, the SA had fifteen thousand soldiers.

Seeing Mussolini's success with the March on Rome, Hitler planned a similar effort to strong-arm his way into the government. His version came in November 1923, about a year after Mussolini's successful march. Hitler planned to seize control of the state government in Munich with his Brownshirts, then

Storm troopers march in Nuremberg in 1929.
[Bundesarchiv, Bild 147-0503 / CC-BY-SA 3.0]

march on Berlin and take down the national government.

But a different drama played out in Germany. While the Italian army stood down when Mussolini marched, the Munich police clashed with the Nazis and crushed the coup attempt, which was later called the Beer Hall Putsch. (The Swiss German word *Putsch* originally meant "knock" or "thrust" but came to mean "coup," a sudden attempt to overthrow a government, because of the numerous attempts to overthrow the Weimar Republic.) Following the failed rebellion, Adolf Hitler was tried for treason and given the lightest possible sentence of five years' imprisonment. Hitler served less than a year, loosely confined in Landsberg Prison, about forty miles west of Munich. He turned thirty-five while in prison, living in furnished quarters more like a drawing room than a cell. Fellow Nazi inmates surrounded him as he outlined his strategies, political plans, and central beliefs in *Mein Kampf* (My Struggle).

The book brought together all the racist and expansionist ideas that had filled his popular beer hall speeches. It was savage, filled with vile racism and vitriolic attacks on Jews, who he alleged were bent on a "Jewish world dictatorship." One of Hitler's biographers, Joachim Fest, once wrote, "A curiously nasty, obscene odor emanates from the pages of *Mein Kampf*."

Following his release from prison, Hitler rebuilt the party around a group of loyal followers who were to remain the center of the Nazi movement and state. Each year, the party would march in a celebratory parade that proudly retraced the steps of the failed putsch.

The putsch failure convinced Hitler that the Nazi movement

could not destroy the Weimar Republic without support from the regular army and police. Any attempt to overthrow the state by force would bring forth a military response in its defense. But the Nazi Party was still a fringe group with little political power. It received only 2.6 percent of the vote in the Reichstag elections of 1928.

In the years that followed, a worldwide economic depression and the rising power of labor unions and Communists, who blamed the financial catastrophe on capitalism, brought fearful Germans to the Nazi ranks. As Hitler amped up his racist and violent message to rapt German audiences, the country

Adolf Hitler, Julius Streicher (foreground, right), and Hermann Göring (left of Hitler) retrace the steps of the 1923 Beer Hall Putsch in Munich, Germany, on November 9, 1934. [U.S. Holocaust Memorial Museum]

was caught in a period of great anger and resentment. Capable of channeling the pent-up fear and frustration into his message, Hitler inspired a passionate following that viewed him as more than an ordinary politician.

His frenzied speeches left audiences thinking he was a German savior who could restore the nation's glories. It was a meeting of a man and a moment. "What Hitler did was advertise unoriginal ideas in an original way," biographer Ian Kershaw writes. "He gave voice to phobias, prejudice, and resentment as no one else could. . . . He learnt, in other words, that he was able to mobilize the masses."

When the stock market crashed in 1929, Germany's economic crisis continued. Widespread debt affected its citizens, unemployment in the iron and steel mills rose, and farmers struggled to keep their land from being sold. The Nazis fed on the disillusionment and despair caused by failing banks, empty food shops, and mass unemployment. From three million to more than four million Germans were unemployed. Ian Kershaw says, "The protest of ordinary people who took the view that democracy had failed them, that 'the system' should be swept away, became shriller."

Hitler seized on the crisis to assail the ineffectiveness of democratic government. He pledged to restore prosperity, create civil order, eliminate the influence of Jewish financiers, and make Germany, the fatherland, a world power once again.

In the July 1932 elections, Hitler's Nazis expanded their electoral victories and emerged as key players in German politics. A few months later, on January 30, 1933, urged by some of

Hitler leads a Nazi rally at Nuremberg in 1928.
[National Archives and Records Administration]

his advisers, the ailing President Hindenburg appointed Hitler chancellor. "That historic day was an end and a beginning," says Kershaw. "Hitler's appointment as Chancellor marked the beginning of the process which was to lead into the abyss of war and genocide. . . . It signified the start of the astonishingly swift jettisoning of constraints on inhumane behavior whose path ended in Auschwitz, Treblinka, Sobibor, Majdanek, and the other death camps whose names are synonymous with the horror of Nazism."

The Reichstag fire in late February 1933 allowed Hitler to seize power legally and undo the personal liberties protected under the Weimar constitution. The fire was blamed on several Communist Party members, left-wing intellectuals, and labor organizers, who were dragged away by Hitler's notorious Brownshirts. Some were beaten and tortured; others were simply murdered. With breathtaking speed, Hitler was in uncontested control of Germany.

Then, on the Night of the Long Knives, Hitler began a sweeping series of arrests and executions. Between June 30 and July 2, 1934, he purged his storm troopers. This was a murderous elimination of any rivals to Hitler's power within the party, including SA leader Ernst Röhm. In this sudden wave of bloodletting, hundreds of party members—possibly as many as a thousand—were killed, and many more beaten, tortured, or thrown into prisons.

TODAY HITLER IS ALL OF GERMANY, proclaimed a headline on August 4, 1934. Two days earlier, Reich president Paul von Hindenburg had died. Hitler abolished the Reich presidency, and members of the regular army were forced to swear an oath of unconditional obedience to "the Führer of the German Reich and People."

Once in complete command, Hitler expanded the army, reintroduced the military draft, and began developing a new air force, all in violation of the 1919 Versailles Treaty. He also strengthened the power of his elite military corps, the SS (short for *Schutzstaffel,* "protective echelon"), and the Gestapo (*Geheime Staatspolizei,* "secret state police"), which operated outside the law or any judicial review. Both groups grew in power and were central to carrying out the Holocaust, responsible for the network of concentration camps and eventual extermination of millions of Jews and others considered "undesirable" by the Nazis.

And German patriotic pride, left crushed by the defeat in World War I, was being restored. In 1936, just a month before the Olympic Games, Hitler had moved German soldiers into a territory called the Rhineland, bordering France. Under the Versailles Treaty of 1919, Germany could not station troops there. But Hitler simply ignored this, baiting France, Britain, and other nations to respond.

His breach of the treaty went unpunished. The German people were ecstatic over this forceful assertion of their rights and power. As he traveled through Germany, Hitler was greeted by adoring crowds. In an election following the Rhineland campaign, his Nazis won 98.9 percent of the vote. While voting laws had made Germany a virtual one-party state, Hitler used the result as evidence of an overwhelming show of popular support for his program to make Germany great again.

Like Mussolini, Hitler also knew that part of his plan for unquestioned loyalty and a German future lay with shaping Germany's young people. While there were other German groups and clubs for children to join, the Youth League of the Nazi Party was organized in the early 1920s and formally named the Hitler Youth in 1926. The League of German Girls, a branch for girls and young women, was created four years later. By the time Hitler became chancellor in January 1933, the Hitler Youth had a hundred thousand members; it had two million by the end of the year.

Over the next three years, other German youth organizations, including religious groups, were forced into the Hitler Youth or stigmatized and eventually forbidden. Some youth leaders were terrorized and fled the country; others were murdered outright. By the end of 1936, there were 5.4 million Hitler Youth, and a March 1939 decree made service in the organization compulsory for everyone between ten and eighteen.

As a symbol of the future, the Hitler Youth were typically present at party rallies and marches, including the annual Nuremberg rally, which attracted massed crowds of uniformed Germans enthralled by the spectacle created around these Nazi meetings. In 1934, sixty thousand Hitler Youth marched into the stadium to salute Hitler, a display carefully orchestrated in part by Leni Riefenstahl, a film director who captured the scene in her landmark *Triumph of the Will*. Acknowledged as one of the most influential films in movie history, it was a piece of pure propaganda, as opposed to a documentary, with scenes staged and reshot for maximum effect. The film was shown repeatedly around the country to those who could not attend in person. "It was the most fascinating thing I could imagine," recalled a man who saw it as a ten-year-old. "He was illuminated and revered: the Führer, *my* Führer."

The Nazi youth movement was about not only preparing for the future but also exerting Nazi control. Any loyalty to the most basic social structures—schools, churches, and scouting groups—were going to be replaced with loyalty to the party. Children were asked to report on what was happening in their communities and even within their families. The much-feared Gestapo, the secret plainclothes police force that had unlimited powers to arrest any Nazi opponents, was actually quite small. According to the U.S. Holocaust Memorial Museum, "In 1944, it employed only 32,000, of whom 18,500 were actually involved in 'policing.' It maximized these small resources through informants and a large number of denunciations from the local population."

Behind the popularity of the Nazi programs lay the belief that Hitler and his party were restoring a superior German race. By aiming hatred at Jews, other religious minorities, and other ethnic groups in Europe, Hitler was creating an image of a master country dominated by a master race. Of course, these ideas are appalling today. But the uncomfortable history is that Nazi Germany's racial laws had been modeled in part on American laws, such as Virginia's 1924 Racial Integrity and Eugenical Sterilization Acts, which aimed to protect "racial purity" in the United States. In 1928, Hitler expressed admiration for the near elimination of Native Americans. In *Mein Kampf*, he said

Hitler Youth practice with rifles in 1933. [Bundesarchiv, Bild]

the United States was making progress toward the creation of a healthy race-based order. He had in mind U.S. immigration laws, such as the nineteenth-century Chinese Exclusion Act and laws that called for quota systems to keep America more "pure." The Nazis also admired the laws that prohibited marriage between whites and Blacks. These so-called miscegenation laws threatened punishment for interracial marriage in thirty states.

Germany officially created its most infamous racial laws in 1935 when the Nuremberg Laws were passed by the Reichstag. The Law for the Protection of German Blood and Honor prohibited not only marriage but also sexual intercourse between Jews and Germans, and forbid the employment of German women under age forty-five in Jewish households. The Reich Citizenship Law declared that only those with German or related blood could be citizens. The passage of these laws marked the beginning of a state-dictated anti-Semitism that had murderous consequences. "They laid the foundation for future antisemitic measures by legally distinguishing between German and Jew," according to the U.S. Holocaust Museum. "For the first time in history, Jews faced persecution not for what they believed, but for who they—or their parents—were by birth. In Nazi Germany, no profession of belief and no act or statement could convert a Jew into a German. Many Germans who had never practiced Judaism or who had not done so for years found themselves caught in the grip of Nazi terror."

To many Germans, laws like these were part of the way that Hitler was rescuing the nation. Massive building programs had

Hitler breaks ground for the new autobahn in 1933.
[Wikimedia Commons]

transformed cities like Berlin into models of modernity. The autobahn, a network of limited-access, high-speed roadways, was created. These projects not only provided employment, but also served as a powerful propaganda tool to show the progress that Germany was making under the Nazis. German automobiles and airplanes, too, were setting new standards for engineering and design.

In November 1938 came one of the most horrific and chilling moments in which the grip of Hitler's ideas and complete control of the Nazi Party were fully displayed. After Germany expelled Polish Jews, a seventeen-year-old Jewish student in Paris shot and killed a German diplomat upon learning of his family's expulsion. Spurred on by storm troopers, mobs of average Germans and members of the Hitler Youth went on a rampage. They set fires to synagogues across Germany and smashed the windows of hundreds of Jewish shops and homes in what became known as Kristallnacht (Night of Broken Glass).

The rioters destroyed 267 synagogues throughout Germany, Austria, and the Sudetenland, a largely German-speaking section of Czechoslovakia. According to the U.S. Holocaust Memorial Museum, "Many synagogues burned throughout the

Germans walk past the Kristallnacht vandalism in November 1938.
[Bundesarchiv, Bild]

night in full view of the public and of local firefighters, who had received orders to intervene only to prevent flames from spreading to nearby buildings. SA and Hitler Youth members across the country shattered the shop windows of an estimated 7,500 Jewish-owned commercial establishments and looted their wares. Jewish cemeteries became a particular object of desecration in many regions."

The expulsion of Polish Jews was all part of the Nazis' plan for the "Aryanization" of Germany, which gained momentum with the 1935 Nuremberg Laws. The violence of Kristallnacht was a large step down the path that led to the extermination of millions of Jews and other "undesirables" in the Final Solution, the death camps of the Holocaust.

This fateful year of 1938 was also when Hitler began his aggressive expansion of national boundaries to incorporate ethnic Germans living outside the country's borders at the time. With the cooperation of Austrian Nazis, he orchestrated the *Anschluss*, the annexation of Austria, in March. Then, at a diplomatic meeting held at Munich in September, representatives of Great Britain and France agreed to allow Germany to occupy the Sudetenland in Czechoslovakia in return for Hitler's pledge not to seek additional territory. Abandoned by its allies, Czechoslovakia had no choice but to submit.

British prime minister Neville Chamberlain, one of the signers of the Munich Agreement, had taken Hitler at his word. Returning to Britain with this agreement in hand, he proudly announced that he had achieved "peace with honor, " adding, "I believe it is peace for our time." The following year, however, the German army simply defied the agreement and swallowed up the rest of Czechoslovakia. Chamberlain has been pilloried ever since as one of the politicians who made the mistake of appeasing Hitler at great cost.

In 1939, Hitler and Italy's Mussolini concluded the Pact of Steel, which formalized a political and military alliance between their two countries. At the same time, Hitler began secret negotiations with the Soviet Union, led by fellow Strongman and Communist leader Joseph Stalin. The two countries made a "nonaggression pact," surprising in that Hitler hated Communists as much as he hated anyone and was pledged to ultimately destroy the "subhuman" Slavic people of Eastern Europe. The pact eliminated a potential military foe, and Hitler felt emboldened to invade Poland in September 1939, triggering World War II.

Once the war began in 1939, the Nazis established ghettos in which Jews were segregated. Thousands of camps and other detention sites were established across Nazi-occupied Europe. The deportation of Jews to these ghettos culminated in the policy of extermination the Nazis called the "Final Solution to the Jewish Question" in 1942. Under directions from the highest Nazi leadership, killings were committed within Germany and throughout occupied Europe, a genocidal wave that continued until the defeat of the Nazis in May 1945. Victims were deported from the ghettos in sealed freight trains to the death camps where those who survived the journey, were killed in gas chambers.

The Holocaust and the Final Solution were grotesque by

every measure, but Hitler did not only want to eradicate the Jews. The crusade he inspired sought to eliminate other religious groups, homosexuals, the handicapped, and people otherwise judged to have "genetic flaws."

He also set out to destroy Poland and the Soviet Union. On June 22, 1941, Hitler broke his pact with Stalin and attacked the Soviet Union in a massive assault code-named Operation Barbarossa. During the war, the Germans murdered about as many non-Jews as Jews, chiefly through starvation of war prisoners and residents of cities under attack, or by shooting more than a million civilians in reprisals for attacks on Germans.

But Hitler sealed his fate when he betrayed the deal with Stalin. Fighting on two fronts, Hitler's armies would ultimately be crushed. His incredible hunger for power ultimately doomed the Strongman.

Among the many young Germans who would be sent to the Russian conflict was a twenty-three-year-old medical student named Hans Scholl. Disillusioned as a member of the Hitler Youth, Scholl had already turned on the Nazi government. Before he left for Russia, Hans and some student friends at the University of Munich had written and distributed a series of leaflets attacking Hitler and the Nazis. The leaflets had appeared in several German cities in June and July of 1942 under the name of the White Rose, an arbitrary symbol representing innocence. The third White Rose leaflet assailed the Nazi "dictatorship of evil." Others called for sabotage of factories. Scholl and his friends knew that their words would carry a death sentence if they were caught.

One of the fortunate survivors of the brutal fighting and deadly conditions of war in the Russian winter, Hans Scholl returned to school in December 1942 having learned of the mass deportations and concentration camps. By 1943, the German war effort on the Eastern Front was collapsing after the Red Army had defeated the Germans in the largest and one of the most deadly battles of the war, the siege of Stalingrad. Leaflet #5 had warned the German people that Hitler was leading the country to disaster. Knowing of the horrific losses and atrocities committed by the Nazis, the White Rose students resumed their work. Hans's twenty-one-year-old sister, Sophie, also a student, had joined them too.

In 1943, the group produced two more leaflets damning the Nazis. The seventh leaflet warned that all of Germany was encircled and that defeat was certain. It then called on Germans to rise up against Hitler's regime.

On the morning of February 18, 1943, Hans and Sophie Scholl set off for the university carrying hundreds of leaflets in a suitcase, despite knowing the enormous risk. The brother and sister distributed them secretly, dropping them outside classroom doors while lectures were still in session.

They hoped that their nation's recent defeats had begun to change the attitudes of young Germans toward the war. Almost finished with their task, Sophie threw the last leaflets into the air from the top of the staircase, letting them fall into the university's grand entrance hall.

A janitor picked them up and spotted the two students. He quickly locked the doors. A few moments later, officers from the

dreaded Gestapo were at the school, and the two students were arrested. Four days later, Hans, Sophie, and Christoph Probst, another member of the White Rose society, were brought into a Munich courtroom. There would be no mercy. All three were quickly convicted and sentenced to death.

On February 22, 1943, Sophie, Hans, and twenty-three-year-old Christoph were all beheaded by guillotine inside a Munich prison. Eventually more than one hundred other suspects were swept up, many of them just because they were friends or family members of the accused. More executions followed, including those of Willi Graf and Alex Schmorell.

The fourth White Rose leaflet, produced in July 1942, had concluded, "We will not be silent. We are your bad conscience. The White Rose will not leave you in peace." British warplanes even dropped copies of the last White Rose leaflet, which had been smuggled out of the country, over German cities and towns. And the White Rose was not the only resistance to Hitler and the Nazis. Other groups were actively—and very secretly—trying to end Hitler's rule, even by assassination. Among the most prominent of these was a group of military men who wanted to kill Hitler and make peace with the Allies.

On July 20, 1944, a bomb detonated in a conference room where Hitler was present, but apart from a shattered eardrum, he was largely unharmed. Among the people linked to the conspirators was a German pastor and writer named Dietrich Bonhoeffer. He was condemned to death and hanged on April 9, 1945, just as the war was coming to an end.

The assassination attempts and the White Rose movement

may have failed, but the students' leaflets that warned that Germany's situation was hopeless turned out to be correct. Stalin's Red Army was advancing toward Germany from the East, intent on avenging the German brutality against Russians and other Eastern Europeans. As Hitler's once invincible armies started to fall back toward the fatherland, British and American warplanes were dropping tons of bombs on the German heartland.

On June 6, 1944, the D-Day invasion of Normandy, France, meant Allied forces were ready to march toward Germany from the west while more than two million men in Stalin's Red Army began advancing on Berlin from the east. There would still be long months of hard, costly combat, but by the spring of 1945, Berlin was under siege.

Hitler was essentially trapped in his underground bunker and experiencing violent mood swings and physical decline. Described as a hypochondriac—someone excessively worried about being ill—Hitler was now taking numerous pills, medicines, and injections, including opiates, to treat gas and intestinal spasms and a host of other symptoms, real or imagined. He may have had a progressive nervous system disorder called Parkinson's disease and was under extreme stress as his world crumbled around him. He still envisioned an offensive to destroy the Allies approaching from the west, but he was running out of soldiers. The German army was forcing old men and young boys into uniform to put up a last-ditch defense.

Germany's coming defeat was the result of what biographer Ian Kershaw described as a "high-stakes 'winner-takes-all'

gamble for continental dominance and world power which the country's leaders—not just Hitler—backed by much of a gullible population had earlier been prepared to take, and which now was costing the country dearly."

In the last days of his Nazi rule, with the Soviet troops advancing into the suburbs of Berlin, Hitler married Eva Braun, his longtime mistress. Then they committed suicide together on April 30, 1945, two days after Mussolini had been executed in Italy.

Adolf Hitler was a monster. "An ill-educated beerhall demagogue and racist bigot, a narcissistic megalomaniac," he led a nation into a war that left fifty million dead and inspired a policy of genocide that haunts the world. Nazi propaganda and a cult of personality made it seem like the work of one man. But he had cultivated like-minded people as devoted followers and then won a country with his promises of restoring a broken nation to greatness. Like all dictators and despots, he had help. Businesspeople, industrialists, civil servants, and the military all supported his aims and ambitions. He had, it has been said, "willing executioners."

No Strongman is an island.

Within hours of Hitler's death, the hammer-and-sickle flag, the symbol of Hitler's greatest nemesis, the Soviet Union, hung over the German capital. Hitler's city and much of his empire in Eastern Europe were now firmly in the hands of another Strongman, the master of the Soviet Union, Joseph Stalin.

Dec. 18, **1878**	Iosif Dzhugashvili, later known as Joseph Stalin, is born in Gori, Georgia.
1912	Stalin becomes editor of *Pravda* (Truth).
Aug. **1914**	World War I begins.
Nov. **1917**	Bolsheviks seize control of the Russian government.
July 17, **1918**	Czar Nicholas II and his family are executed.
1922	Stalin is appointed general secretary of the Communist Party.
1928	First Five-Year Plan collectivizing agriculture begins.
1932-1933	Holodomor: The mass starvation of Ukrainian peasants takes place.
1937-1938	The Great Purge: Rivals to Stalin's power are eliminated through executions, exile, and imprisonment; deaths are estimated in the millions.
Aug. 23, **1939**	Germany and Soviet Union sign Molotov-Ribbentrop Pact, a treaty of nonaggression.
Sept. 1, **1939**	Germany invades Poland, triggering World War II.
Sept. 17, **1939**	Soviet Union invades Poland from the east.
June 22, **1941**	Operation Barbarossa: Germany invades the Soviet Union.
Feb. **1945**	The Yalta Conference: Stalin, Winston Churchill, and Franklin D. Roosevelt make plans to divide the occupied Germany.
May 2, **1945**	Berlin falls to Stalin's Red Army.

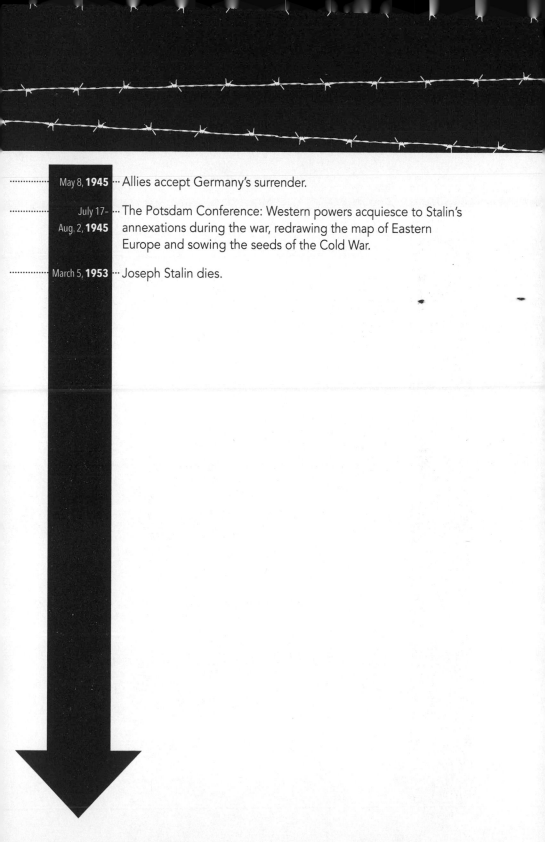

May 8, **1945**	Allies accept Germany's surrender.
July 17– Aug. 2, **1945**	The Potsdam Conference: Western powers acquiesce to Stalin's annexations during the war, redrawing the map of Eastern Europe and sowing the seeds of the Cold War.
March 5, **1953**	Joseph Stalin dies.

MAN OF STEEL

Soviet leader Joseph Stalin, U.S. President Franklin D. Roosevelt, and UK Prime Minister Winston Churchill met in Iran in 1943 to coordinate their plans to defeat the Nazis in World War II. After the war with Germany ended, the Cold War between Stalin's Soviet Union and the western democracies began. [Library of Congress]

THE STORY OF JOSEPH STALIN

Shukhov was in for treason. He'd admitted it under investigation. . . . The counterespionage boys had beaten the hell out of him. The choice was simple enough: don't sign and dig your own grave, or sign and live a bit longer. He signed.

—**Aleksandr Solzhenitsyn,** *One Day in the Life of Ivan Denisovich*

• • •

By his word he could kill them, have them tortured, have them rescued again, have them rewarded. . . . Life and death depended on his whim.

—**Erich Fromm,** *The Anatomy of Human Destructiveness*

• • •

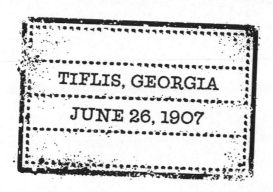

TIFLIS, GEORGIA
JUNE 26, 1907

IT SEEMED LIKE AN ordinary morning in Tiflis, a lively market town in Georgia, part of the vast Russian Empire. Young women carrying parasols strolled the square lined with shops, a grand hotel, and the state bank. Two horse-drawn carriages rolled into the square, guarded by fierce Cossacks. With their woolen hats and curved sabers, Cossacks were legendary for their fighting ability.

Without warning, two women dropped their parasols and tossed grenades beneath the carriages. At the same instant, shots rang out as gunmen on the street and the surrounding rooftops began firing weapons. As the grenades exploded, the horses fell and the carriages came to a halt. Then one horse jumped up and bolted away in a panic, dragging its carriage behind, only to be killed by more grenades.

The peaceful morning erupted in carnage as bullets ripped through both carriages, killing two passengers. The mounted Cossacks fell, bleeding in the street. The hail of gunfire cut down police officers as they rushed to the scene. Disguised as an officer, a bandit collected several sacks of money from the

Tiflis in 1901. [Wikimedia Commons]

coaches and made a getaway in his own carriage.

This might have looked like some run-of-the-mill stagecoach holdup, typical of old Hollywood Westerns. But at least forty people died in the spectacular robbery. The carriages that were attacked belonged to the czar, ruler of the Russian Empire, and the thieves were not just any bank robbers. The bandit with the moneybags turned the loot over to the robbery's mastermind, a man later known to the world as Joseph Stalin. The stolen money, worth an equivalent of three million dollars, had been promised to Communist leader Vladimir Lenin to help finance the revolution he was trying to rouse across the vast country.

From revolutionary bank robber to Russian Communist Party leader and eventual master of the Soviet Union, Stalin was a brutal and murderous Strongman, in war and peace. Even his surname, which he chose for himself, meant "man of steel" in Russian. At the time of his death in March 1953, Stalin had transformed the Soviet Union into a twentieth-century world power that helped defeat Hitler, developed nuclear weapons, and started a rocket program that launched Sputnik, the first man-made satellite, into space in 1957, a few years after he died. Stalin built a Soviet-dominated empire in Eastern Europe and challenged the United States during the Cold War. He remains

The Cossack cavalry fought for Russia in 1915. [Wikimedia Commons]

one of the most influential figures in modern history. Yet Stalin was a ruthless killer of millions.

"Russia is still struggling whether to view him as mass murderer or a national hero," writes Samuel Rachlin, a journalist born in Siberia after his Lithuanian family was deported there in 1941, as Stalin's iron-fisted rule spread across Eastern Europe. "Although Russians know more about Stalin's crimes than they did ever before, many politicians and historians want to pull him out of the shadows and celebrate him for his role in the industrialization of the young Soviet state and the victory over Nazi Germany. . . . Russians have never been able to agree on how they should view Stalin."

Joseph Stalin was born Iosif Vissarionovich Dzhugashvili in the peasant village of Gori, Georgia, on December 18, 1878. His father, Vissarion, was a poor cobbler, and his mother was a washerwoman named Ekaterina, known as Keke. They had two children who both died in infancy, one of measles, before Joseph was born. Nicknamed Soso, he was said to be a frail child. At age seven, Joseph survived a bout of smallpox, a killer disease that ravaged the world for many centuries before it was eradicated through vaccination.

Known as Mad Beso, Joseph's father was a harsh, hard-drinking man who thrashed his son regularly. Eventually he lost his shoe business and went to work in a Tiflis shoe factory. Keke, a devout Russian Orthodox woman, wanted her son to become a priest. In 1888, she enrolled him in Gori's church school. Bright, though not an outstanding student, Joseph taught himself Russian and did well enough to win a scholarship to the theological seminary in Tiflis, where he was enrolled in 1894 at age fifteen.

While studying for the Orthodox priesthood, the teenage Soso met a secret group at the seminary whose members sought Georgia's independence from czarist Russia. Some of the members were also Socialists, and they introduced Soso to the works of Karl Marx, the influential

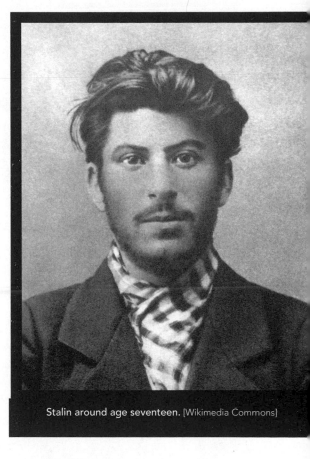

Stalin around age seventeen. [Wikimedia Commons]

German author of *Das Kapital* and *The Communist Manifesto*. He would also be introduced to the ideas and writings of Tulin, a pseudonym of Vladimir Ilyich Ulyanov, who later took the alias Lenin. Stalin once said, "If there'd been no Lenin, I'd have stayed a choirboy and seminarian."

Born in 1870, Lenin had emerged as the leader of the Russian revolutionary movement in the late nineteenth century. As a young man, he had been expelled from the imperial Kazan University for protesting the Russian Empire's czarist government. In 1897, he had been exiled to Siberia for

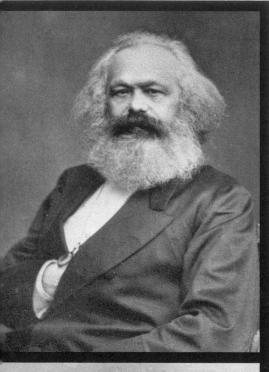

The Fathers of Communism: Karl Marx
in 1875 and Vladimir Lenin in Switzerland
during his exile in 1916. [Wikimedia Commons]

sedition—inciting people to rebel against the state. A Marxist true believer, Lenin lived by the Communist credo: "Workers of the world, unite!" The chief political theorist of Russian Communism, Lenin wanted more than a Russian revolution. He was dedicated to the worldwide overthrow of capitalism, to be replaced with Marxist Socialism. The Russian Social-Democratic Workers' Party eventually split into two factions. Lenin led one of these, known as the Bolsheviks, which ultimately became the Russian Communist Party.

Soso was won over. Although he would not meet Lenin in person for several more years, he threw his lot in with the hardcore Marxist revolutionaries who followed Lenin. Soso joined the rebels at the seminary in 1898, and although he received good marks in school, he left a year later. Official school records stated he was unable to pay the tuition and withdrew. Others say he left because of the ill health of his doting mother. Most likely, he was forced to leave due to his growing radicalism, challenging the regime of Czar Nicholas II. Without a degree and with few prospects, he secured a job as a clerk at the Physical Observatory in Tiflis. Each day, he had to record the weather and temperature four times.

Short and wiry, Soso cast his lot in with the revolutionary underground. Marked by a shock of thick black hair and fierce eyes, he was a powerful presence who began organizing laborers in protests at Georgian factories around 1900. Arrested for coordinating a labor strike, Soso was exiled to Siberia in 1902. The Russian government regularly sent prisoners to work in harsh internal exile in the vast land east of the Ural Mountains, known for its brutally cold winters.

It was the first of more arrests, imprisonments, and Siberian exiles to come. Between 1902 and 1913, Soso was arrested seven times for revolutionary activities, and the czar's secret police marked him as an outlaw for planning robberies, kidnappings, and extortion to finance the revolution.

In later years, he referred to those violent times as playing "Cossacks and bandits," writes biographer Simon Montefiore, "the Russian version of 'cops and robbers.' . . . Always on the move, often on the run, he used the many uniforms of Tsarist society as his disguises, and frequently escaped manhunts by dressing in drag."

His philosophy can be summed up in two expressions:

"Might makes right" and "The end justifies the means." Or as Stalin biographer Robert Service puts it, "Radical Marxists anticipated civil war between the middle classes and the working classes on a global scale. From such a conflict would come good for following generations. Marxism justified the sacrifice of millions of human beings in the pursuit of revolution. The perfect society was anticipated once the military conflict was ended. The poor would inherit the earth."

It was during this time that Soso plotted the spectacular holdup in Tiflis to "expropriate" funds for Lenin's Bolshevik Party. Around 1912, he adopted the name Stalin, and the Man of Steel was assigned to edit the Bolshevik newspaper *Pravda*

Joseph Stalin, apparently taken during his exile in Siberia in 1915. [Wikimedia Commons]

(Truth). After another robbery attempt failed, Stalin was hunted down by imperial police and arrested in 1913. Yet again, he was condemned to four years for revolutionary activities and sent to Turukhansk, Siberia, where conditions were worse than those of his first remote exile had been. According to biographer Simon Montefiore, "It was harsher and more desolate than anything the Georgian had experienced before. He was soon at the lowest ebb of his life. Daily life in Turukhansk was meant to be a struggle. . . . Many exiles out there perished from the extremities of weather. By early November, it was –33°, heading to –55°. Saliva froze on the lips, breath crystallized."

This time, Stalin's exile in Siberia ended during a turning point in Russian history. Russia was suffering severely from food shortages and terrible battlefield losses in the Great War. With the country in chaos and shops empty of bread, people filled the streets shouting, "Down with the czar!" In March 1917, army regiments began to mutiny. Some sixty thousand soldiers joined the armed rebellion, and Czar Nicholas II was forced to abdicate.

Russia's record in the war had largely been a string of disasters, almost from the outset in August 1914. In a loss to the Germans at the Battle of Tannenberg, ninety-two thousand Russian soldiers were captured in one of the worst military defeats by any army during the war. More than two million Russian soldiers were killed in the war, along with millions of civilians — one of many reasons that the Russian people as well as Russian armies were ready to bring an end to czarist rule.

When the czar abdicated (gave up his power), a weak provisional government attempted to create a new Russian republic with an elected legislature. This attempt at new democratic leadership, plagued from the outset by resistance from Lenin's militant Bolsheviks, lasted only about eight months. Having grabbed control in Russia's largest cities, the Bolsheviks introduced Communist rule and seized complete power over Russia in the Bolshevik Revolution of November 1917.

King George V of England (left) and Czar Nicholas II of Russia in Berlin in 1913, the year before World War I broke out. [Wikimedia Commons]

Returning after a decade in exile for his revolutionary acts, Lenin pulled Bolshevik-controlled Russia out of the world war. He had returned home in a train provided by the German kaiser and then made a treaty with Germany on March 3, 1918. Under its terms, the new Soviet government—the word *soviet* simply meant "council"—recognized the independence of neighboring countries Ukraine, Georgia, and Finland, previously controlled by Russia. Poland and the Baltic states of Lithuania, Latvia, and Estonia were surrendered to Germany and Austria-Hungary. Other territories were ceded to Turkey. In total, the treaty surrendered some one million square miles of Russia's former territory. After the war ended with Germany's defeat in November 1918, those territories became independent.

The Bolsheviks took control of Moscow's ancient fortress known as the Kremlin and converted it into the headquarters of the Soviet government, and it eventually became synonymous with the Communist dictatorship. But even as Lenin took control of what had been the czar's empire after the Bolshevik Revolution, other Russian groups fought back. They included supporters of the former monarchy, landowners, business leaders, and capitalists—with support from foreign governments, including the United States—who still hoped to create a democratic republic in Russia. For the next few years, Russia and much of Eastern Europe were caught in a bloody civil war that was one of the most costly conflicts in European history. It would continue until 1922, when the Bolsheviks gained complete control.

The hammer and sickle, symbol of the Bolshevik Revolution,

would soon fly over Russia—or what came to be the Soviet Union. Following the 1917 Revolution, four socialist republics were established on territory of the former empire: the Russian and Transcaucasian Soviet Federated Socialist Republics and the Ukrainian and Belorussian Soviet Socialist Republics.

On December 30, 1922, these groups formed the Union of Soviet Socialist Republics (USSR)—the Soviet Union—a vast new empire that spread across Europe into Asia, from the Baltic Ocean to the Pacific. The hammer represented the factory workers, and the sickle stood for the peasant farmers. United, they would create Marx's "dictatorship of the proletariat"—the word *proletariat* essentially meaning "laborers" or "the working class" and another vestige of ancient Rome, where *proletariat* applied to people with no property. The idea was to create a "workers' paradise" in which the old forms of society were wiped away and every citizen would be entitled to free education, work, food, shelter, and health care.

There would be no paradise, however, for those Russians whose world had been turned upside down. As the brutal civil war was being waged, Czar Nicholas II and his family had remained prisoners. His fortified Moscow

The hammer and sickle, which became the symbol of Soviet rule.
[Wikimedia Commons]

palace, the Kremlin, had become the center of the new Communist powers, and Lenin and Stalin both lived in what was once the palace of the czar. In the early hours of July 17, 1918, Czar Nicholas, his wife, Alexandra, their five children (four girls and a boy), and four servants were awakened and ordered to dress quickly and go down to the cellar of the house in Yekaterinburg in which they were being held. But then an execution order was read, and a dozen armed men began firing on the family. Jewels sewn into the corsets of the girls, to help pay for a possible escape, deflected the bullets, prompting the executioners to stab them with bayonets.

The Romanov dynasty of three hundred years had come to a gruesome end. The executioners had apparently planned to destroy or disfigure the bodies with acid, but that plan was not carried out. The bones of the parents, Czar Nicholas II and Czarina Alexandra, and three of their daughters were exhumed in 1991. In 2008, DNA evidence confirmed that the remains of a boy and a girl found the year before in a grave in Yekaterinburg, where the execution took place, belonged to Crown Prince Aleksei and another of his sisters. The violence that took the lives of the Romanovs was a foreboding omen of the bloodletting to come in the fight for control of Russia.

During the years of revolution, Stalin had occupied a series of fairly low-level party jobs. Lenin thought Stalin was ill educated and rough edged, but he had proved his loyalty and value as a bank robber. In 1922, Stalin was appointed to another such post, as general secretary of the Communist Party's Central Committee. He used his new position to consolidate power in exactly this way—by controlling all appointments and access to Lenin.

By placing his friends and allies in powerful positions—what is called cronyism—Stalin built a base of power for a future dictatorship that would last until his death in 1953. Nearly all members of the central command eventually owed their place to him. Even Lenin, gravely ill after suffering a stroke, was helpless to regain control from Stalin before his death in 1924. After Lenin's death, Stalin further strengthened his steely grip by eliminating his chief rival to power, Leon Trotsky, one of the central leaders of the Russian Revolution. Trotsky lost the power struggle and was exiled from Russia. He was assassinated in Mexico City in 1940 on Stalin's orders.

While some thought he was merely a "dumb thug," Stalin had grand ambitions and an endless appetite for power. Determined to transform the Soviet Union at any cost, he created a series of five-year economic plans designed to turn a nation of peasant farmers into a twentieth-century industrial power. Central to the first Five-Year Plan was "collectivization," which meant the state would control *everything*. Private property ceased to exist.

Stalin's collectivization became an incredibly harsh, violent, and wrenching nightmare. Rural peasants were only a generation removed from serfdom, a system under which they were little different from enslaved people. In 1861, more than twenty-three million serfs had been freed from their lords when serfdom was abolished. Under Stalin, the former serfs were forced to join communal farms or work in state factories.

Hundreds of thousands of kulaks, peasants who had become

An ailing Lenin meets with Stalin in 1922.
[Wikimedia Commons]

wealthy enough to purchase their own farms, were rounded up and executed, their lands confiscated. Those who owned some land or livestock were stripped of their property, simply because the Soviet idea was to end private property. Of course, many of these kulaks resisted and were then considered "counterrevolutionary." Amid confusion and resistance to collectivization in the countryside, agricultural productivity dropped. The grain that was produced went to the state. Devastating food shortages followed, and millions died in Russia and Ukraine during the Great Famine of 1932–1933.

"At the height of the crisis," historian Anne Applebaum writes, "organized teams of policemen and party activists, motivated by hunger, fear, and a decade of hateful and conspiratorial rhetoric, entered peasant households and took everything edible: potatoes, beets, squash, beans, peas, anything in the oven and anything in the cupboard, farm animals and pets. The

A parade of Russian peasants stand under a banner that reads, "We will liquidate the kulaks as a class." [Wikimedia Commons]

result was a catastrophe: at least 5 million people perished of hunger between 1931 and 1934 all across the Soviet Union. Among them were more than 3.9 million Ukrainians. The famine of 1932–3 was described in émigré publications at the time and later as the *Holodomor*, a word derived from the Ukrainian words for hunger—*holod*—and extermination—*mor*."

During World War II, a Polish legal scholar gave a new name to these policies and others like them, in which whole nations or ethnic groups are essentially murdered—*genocide*. Raphael Lemkin combined the Greek word *genos*, meaning "race" or "tribe," with the Latin *cide*, meaning "killing," to coin the new word. *Genocide*, as legally defined by the United Nations in 1948, in language shaped by the Soviet Union, "means any of the following acts committed with intent to destroy, in whole or in part, a national, ethnical, racial or religious group, as such":

- Killing members of the group;
- Causing serious bodily or mental harm to members of the group;
- Deliberately inflicting on the group conditions of life calculated to bring about its physical destruction in whole or in part;
- Imposing measures intended to prevent births within the group;
- Forcibly transferring children of the group to another group.

In practice, the term *genocide* came to mean "the physical elimination of an entire ethnic group in a manner similar to the Holocaust," according to Anne Applebaum. But by Lemkin's original definition, the Holodomor was an act of genocide.

Soon after the enormous death toll of the Great Famine, Stalin began what is known as the Great Terror or the Great Purge. From 1937 to 1938, hundreds of thousands of people were accused of various political crimes such as espionage or the all-purpose "anti-Soviet activities." With show trials or no legal process at all, many were quickly shot. Those spared instant death were dispatched to the forced-labor camp system, called the Gulag, in which millions died of starvation, disease, exposure, and overwork.

The goal was murderously simple: eliminate any threats to Stalin and the Kremlin leadership. "Stalin started and maintained the movement toward the Great Terror," says biographer Robert Service. "He and nobody else was the engineer of imprisonment, torture, penal labor, and shooting. . . . When he acted, his brutality was as mechanical as a badger trap."

In 1939, Stalin was named "Man of the Year" by *Time* magazine, a reminder that the award does not necessarily honor the greatest person, but the one with the greatest impact. Adolf Hitler was "Man of the Year" in 1938. In naming Stalin, the magazine said, "Joseph Stalin has gone a long way toward deifying himself while alive. No flattery is too transparent, no compliment too broad for him. He became the fountain of all Socialist wisdom." It was the first of two such selections, as Stalin was also recognized as "Man of the Year" in 1942.

By early 1939, Soviet prisons and labor camps were already bursting with about eight million people. During the two years of the Great Terror, about one in twenty people in the Soviet

Union had been arrested. Of those arrested, 90 percent would perish. Between 1937 and 1938 alone, one and a half million people were executed and two million more died in the camps. During all of Stalin's dictatorship, as many as eighteen million people may have been sentenced to the Gulag, historians believe, while up to ten million peasants died or were killed in the collectivization of the early 1930s.

And these numbers do not include the losses in the Great Patriotic War, the name the Soviets gave World War II. Against the brutal backdrop of Stalin's starvations and purges, war clouds rose over Europe in 1939. Despite warnings that Germany was mobilizing its forces and that Hitler was intent upon crushing the Soviet Union, Stalin agreed to a nonaggression pact with the Nazis. So, two weeks after Hitler invaded Poland from the west in 1939, Stalin felt he could safely invade Poland from the east.

But Hitler broke the agreement with Stalin. Keen to control Eastern Europe's coal, oil, and vast agricultural lands, Hitler launched his invasion of the Soviet Union—given the code name Operation Barbarossa—in June 1941. Some four million German and Italian soldiers marched into the Soviet Union, the largest invasion in the history of war. As they moved through Poland, Eastern Europe, and the Soviet republics, the Nazis brought their concentration camps, slave labor, and horrific assaults on the soldiers and civilians they were out to conquer.

"The Holocaust overshadows German plans that envisioned even more killing," historian Timothy Snyder writes. "Hitler wanted not only to eradicate the Jews; he wanted also to destroy Poland and the Soviet Union as states, exterminate their ruling classes, and kill tens of millions of Slavs (Russians, Ukrainians, Belarusians, Poles). If the German war against Stalin's Soviet Union had gone as planned, thirty million civilians would have been starved in its first winter, and tens of millions more expelled, killed, assimilated, or enslaved thereafter. Though these plans were never realized, they supplied the moral premises of German occupations policy in the East."

Confronted by Hitler's massive invasion and the potential destruction of the Soviet Union, Stalin joined the Allies in 1941. The United States was not yet in the war, but President Franklin D. Roosevelt agreed to provide military assistance to the Soviets. When the United States declared war on Germany and Japan in December 1941, the United States and the Soviet Union became full partners in the crusade to stop Hitler. Eventually, the United States, Great Britain, and other allies attacked Germany from the west, and the Soviet Union moved on the Nazis from the east.

After a long struggle of nearly unprecedented brutality to fend off the Nazi invasion, Stalin got the opportunity to exact revenge. He attacked Germany without mercy, unleashing the full, fearsome fury of the Red Army on a bombed-out Berlin. Fueled on vodka doled out by Stalin's commanders, the Soviet armies were out to avenge the deaths of some twenty-seven million people, including sixteen million civilians, killed during Operation Barbarossa.

The fall of Berlin in the spring of 1945 remains one of the most grotesque chapters in the brutal history of World War II.

Stalin had pitted his generals against one another, daring them to be the first into Berlin. He expected them to be savage in exacting revenge on Hitler's Germany. When they flew the hammer and sickle over the Reichstag, Hitler's Third Reich was finished.

The Soviet conquest of the Nazis altered the course of world history. Under the Allies' agreement, the occupation of Germany was divided into four zones, controlled separately by the United States, Great Britain, France, and the Soviet Union.

Berlin in ruins after the Battle of Berlin in 1945.
[Alamy]

Berlin, in the Soviet zone, was also divided. With East Germany and East Berlin under Stalin's control, the division would become the hot-button center of Cold War intrigue for much of the next half century.

Stalin began installing Communist governments in the areas his Red Army had liberated from the Nazis, and Eastern Europe fell under the Soviet thumb. From the Kremlin in Moscow, Stalin's henchmen ruled these captive nations with an iron fist, using every fear tactic and familiar tool of repression: secret police, neighborhood informants, state control of the media, and the eradication of individual freedoms. Democratic institutions such as courts and legislatures were replaced by a Soviet-mandated police state. All private property became state property. And always in the background was the presence of tanks ready to roll to do the regime's bidding.

The well-practiced Strongman technique of creating a new generation of loyal young people also had a Soviet face. The Young Pioneers, a Communist scouting group for ages nine to fifteen first organized under Lenin, grew and expanded under Stalin, their "great Leader and Teacher," according to Eugene Yelchin, a Pioneer whose family later escaped the Soviet Union.

"To arrest so many innocent people, crimes had to be invented," Yelchin writes. "Stalin's propaganda machine deceived ordinary people into believing that countless spies and terrorists threatened their security. Tormented by fear, Soviet citizens clung to Stalin for guidance and protection, and soon his popularity reached cult status. 'The father of all Soviet children' smiled and waved at his supporters during parades and celebrations, while at night, in his Kremlin office, he was signing orders for innocent people to be shot without trial."

Among the people swallowed up by Stalin's police state was Aleksandr Solzhenitsyn, a Red Army soldier who was sentenced to ten years in prison for writing letters to a friend that were critical of Stalin. He later described life in a Soviet labor camp in the 1962 novel *One Day in the Life of Ivan Denisovich*. The 1970 Nobel Prize winner also wrote *The Gulag Archipelago*, a 1973 work of nonfiction describing the vast system of labor prisons in which ordinary criminals and Soviet dissidents—including writers, professors, and other intellectuals—were kept in slave labor.

"Ideology—that is what gives evildoing its long-sought justification and gives the evildoer the necessary steadfastness and determination. That is the social theory which helps to make his acts seem good instead of bad in his own and others' eyes. . . . That was how the agents of the Inquisition fortified their wills: by invoking Christianity; the conquerors of foreign lands, by extolling the grandeur of their Motherland; the colonizers, by civilization; the Nazis, by race. . . . Without evildoers there would have been no Archipelago."

Long after his death, Joseph Vissarionovich Stalin, son of a poor Georgian cobbler and his deeply religious wife, had secured a place in history as a dominant figure of the twentieth century. As with Hitler, Stalin can rightfully be called killer, monster, and fiend. But as Robert Service points out, "The lesson to be learned from studying several of the twentieth century's most murderous politicians is that it is wrong to depict them as beings wholly incomparable to ourselves. Not only is it wrong: it is also dangerous. If the likes of Stalin . . . are represented as having been 'animals,' 'monsters,' or 'killing machines,' we shall never be able to discern their successors."

TIME LINE—
THE LIFE OF MAO ZEDONG

Dec. 26, **1893** ··· Mao Zedong is born in Shaoshan, Hunan province.

1911 ··· Army troops rebel, beginning the Chinese Revolution.

Feb. 12, **1912** ··· Xuantong, last emperor of the Qing Dynasty, which ruled China for 267 years, is forced to abdicate, ending more than 2,000 years of imperial rule.

Oct. 16, **1934** ··· Long March begins; Red Army walks six thousand miles.

1939–1945 ··· World War II: Chinese Nationalist and Communist armies fight the Japanese.

March **1943** ··· Mao becomes chairman of the Chinese Communist Party, effectively its supreme leader.

Oct. 1, **1949** ··· People's Republic of China is founded.

Feb. 14, **1950** ··· Mao and Stalin sign Sino-Soviet Treaty of Friendship.

1950–1952 ··· Land reform leads to mass executions of landlords and their families.

1950–1953 ··· Korean War takes place.

1958–1960 ··· The Great Leap Forward: organizes peasants into collective farms with disastrous results, including mass starvation.

Oct. 12, **1964** ··· China successfully detonates its first atomic bomb.

1966 ··· The Cultural Revolution begins and lasts for ten years, during which millions are persecuted, tortured, or killed.

Feb. 21–28, **1972** ··· President Nixon visits China.

Sept. 9, **1976** ··· Mao Zedong dies.

CHAPTER

★ ★ ★ **6** ★ ★ ★

THE LONG MARCH

Red Guards in Tiananmen Square hold copies of Chairman Mao Zedong's Little Red Book during a parade in June 1966 at the beginning of China's Cultural Revolution. More than one million people are believed to have died during the decade-long upheaval. [Wikimedia Commons]

THE STORY
OF
MAO ZEDONG

A revolution is not a dinner party, or writing an essay, or painting a picture, or doing embroidery. . . . A revolution is an insurrection, an act of violence by which one class overthrows another.

—Mao Zedong

• • •

During Mao [Zedong's] Tse-tung's crazy drive to purge all his political enemies, millions died bloodly and many more were wrongly imprisoned. Factories were closed as workers rushed into the streets to shout "Long live Chairman Mao," and schools were shut as Mao stirred youngsters to beat up their teachers, burn down the temples and destroy the ancient arts, and even turn against their own parents in the devilish hunt for more victims.

—Da Chen, *China's Son*

• • •

We can find common ground, despite our differences, to build a world structure in which both can be safe to develop in our own way on our own roads. That cannot be said about some other nations in the world.

—Richard Nixon to Mao Zedong

• • •

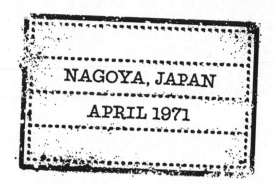

NAGOYA, JAPAN
APRIL 1971

IT WAS THE Ping-Pong shot heard round the world.

Sports had obviously been important to Mussolini and Hitler. And under Stalin and Communist Party leaders, the Soviet Union and its eastern European allies had shown they would use any means necessary to build Olympic teams that proved the superiority of their Communist rule.

But it can be safely said that no sporting event in modern history was as significant as a table tennis tournament held in April 1971. The U.S. table tennis team traveled to Japan for the World Table Tennis Championships. Also in attendance was a team from the People's Republic of China—among the first athletes permitted to leave the rigidly controlled Communist nation in decades. After sending one swimmer to the Helsinki games in 1952, the People's Republic did not send athletes to the Olympics again until 1980. A closed society, Communist China allowed few outsiders in.

When a nineteen-year-old U.S. player boarded a bus carrying the Chinese national team, it was awkward. The two countries were enemies. Since 1949, when the People's Republic of China was born, the countries had been rivals in the cold and hot wars between Communism and Western democracies. During the Korean War of 1950–1953, the United States and China had come terrifyingly close to a nuclear war. And in 1971, the Vietnam War was still raging, with China supporting the North Vietnamese Communists and the United States backing the South Vietnamese.

Glenn Cowan, an admitted hippie, tried to defuse the tension by talking through an interpreter. "I know all this," he began, "my hat, my hair, my clothes look funny to you." He was met with silence. The Chinese team had been told to only greet Americans politely. But then the Chinese team's best player came forward and shook the young American's hand, and Cowan made a spontaneous comment that he would like to see China. The players later exchanged gifts, and Cowan gave the Chinese player a T-shirt printed with the Beatles'"Let It Be."

In Mao Zedong's China, there were no secrets. A report of this meeting was relayed back to the Communist Party leadership. The brief encounter soon led to a stunning surprise. The American team would be welcomed to China and take part in a series of table tennis matches around the country. The invitation could only have come with the blessing of China's uncontested leader, its Strongman, Chairman Mao Zedong.

This was not a casual decision. At that moment, China and its longtime ally, the Soviet Union, were no longer so friendly. Differences in ideology had driven a wedge between the two countries. China had detonated an atomic bomb in 1964, and by

1969, there were border clashes between the two Communist superpowers. Armies of both nations were massed on their shared border.

With the looming possibility of a much wider conflict, the Chinese leadership sought to open the door to the Soviet Union's Cold War foe, the United States. American politicians were eager to widen a split between its two longtime adversaries, China and the Soviet Union. Even before he became president, Richard M. Nixon had written: "We simply cannot afford to leave China forever outside the family of nations."

U.S. president Richard Nixon attends an exhibition table tennis match in Beijing in February 1972. [National Archives]

For most Americans, Ping-Pong was a casual hobby, practiced in suburban basements or school gyms. It was hardly a major international sport and wouldn't become an Olympic event until 1988. But these Ping-Pong games became a diplomatic breakthrough that changed history.

Touring China for a week, the American team played a series of exhibition matches in which keeping score hardly mattered. The gracious Chinese hosts allowed their guests to win their share of games. But by the time the Americans left on April 17, a simple game featuring paddles and little white balls had begun to shift the world's balance of power. A Chinese team was later invited to America.

This Ping-Pong diplomacy—made famous again in 1994 when the fictional Forrest Gump, played by Tom Hanks, joined the American team visiting China—soon led to a more earth-shaking announcement: President Richard Nixon was going to visit the People's Republic.

Today, Chinese students attend American universities. American tourists flock to such sites as the Great Wall of China. Chinese-manufactured products from baby toys to smartphones and computers fill American stores. And American businesses have eagerly sought a foothold in the world's largest consumer market. But in 1972, no sitting U.S. president had ever set foot in mainland China, which was a resolute enemy of the United States. The fact that *Richard Nixon* was going to the Communists was what made the news so extraordinary. Elected president in 1968, Nixon had built his political career as a hardline anti-Communist. As a congressman, he had solidified his anti-Communist reputation as he led a dogged quest to expose American Communists and Soviet spies during the late 1940s. As Dwight Eisenhower's vice president in 1959, Nixon made headlines by challenging Soviet leader Nikita Khrushchev at a Moscow display of a typical U.S. model home filled with consumer goods available to most Americans. Their televised exchange went down in history as the "Kitchen Debate" and gained Nixon more popularity, although he lost the 1960 presidential election to John F. Kennedy.

And then there was Mao. In 1972, it was well known that Mao Zedong was a ruthless leader whose policies, like Stalin's, had led to the deaths of millions of Chinese people through starvation, imprisonment, torture, and execution.

As part of a trip that Nixon called "the week that changed the world," the U.S. president met and shook hands with Chairman Mao Zedong. Describing this historic encounter, which led to normalizing relations, biographer Philip Short wrote, "One of them presided over the citadel of international capitalism, backed by the strongest economy and military forces in the world; the other was uncontested patriarch of a revolutionary communist state of 800 million people, whose ideology called for the overthrow of capitalism wherever it might appear. The photograph in the *People's Daily* next day told China, and the world, that the global balance of power had been transformed."

As amazing as it was for Americans to see, this extraordinary meeting was almost unimaginable to a people who had been largely cut off from the Western world for centuries. The

President Nixon meets Chairman Mao Zedong in February 1972.
[National Archives]

Chinese were the heirs of an ancient civilization that had built a wall to keep out foreigners. In many ways, they still lived behind that wall. And the Strongman who ruled with an iron fist was now shaking hands with a longtime enemy.

Mao Zedong was born in a village of rice farmers on the nineteenth day of the eleventh month of the Year of the Snake by the ancient Chinese calendar—or December 26, 1893. His father, Mao Rensheng, was born a peasant, but he served as a soldier and used his earnings to buy farmland in Shaoshan, a remote village in the rice-growing province of Hunan. Mao Rensheng was a prosperous man by Chinese standards of the day, and he became a landlord by buying up the mortgages of other peasants.

As a small boy, Mao was required to help with farm chores, like tending the ducks and helping with the harvest. At age eight, Mao started his schooling. He was expected to get a basic education that would be useful in running the family's farm business. For a Chinese boy at the time, education meant rote learning of the strict values of Confucianism, the ancient system of morals, behavior, and ethics that had dictated Chinese society for centuries. One of the fundamental Confucian ideas was of a strong, centralized state with a wise, paternalistic ruler.

Just as Western students were forced for centuries to copy and read ancient Greek and Latin texts, Chinese education emphasized the rigors of reciting the Confucian texts and then writing them down in precise characters. Mao later admitted that he didn't enjoy the classical Chinese texts preaching Confucian morals. But for a boy who dreamed of leaving behind his life in a rice-farming village, an education was the way out. By passing certain tests, a young man might gain a post in the Chinese imperial government.

From a young age, Mao showed a rebellious streak, and was expelled from several schools before he was fourteen. He rattled China's strict conventions even more dramatically when he walked out on an arranged marriage at age fourteen. Mao's father had set up his teenage son with the teenage daughter of a relative. For Chinese teenagers at the time, such an arrangement was not unusual. However, defying your parents was shameful and shocking. Although the marriage was official, Mao later said he never considered the young woman, known as Miss Luo, to be his wife. (Although Mao left home and stayed with a friend, Miss Luo may have remained in the Mao family's household for several years before she died.)

The teenager's open refusal of his father's wishes was extremely daring—an act that might have meant being disowned or severely punished. But Mao had no regrets, saying later, "I learned that when I defended my rights by open rebellion my father relented, but when I remained weak and submissive he only beat me more."

Was this act of rebellion a sign of things to come? One biographer of Mao says, "The youth of sixteen had become a very Chinese kind of rebel in a very particular moment of historical change. . . . He lashed out less at his father than what his father stood for." Despite his defiance, Mao was sent to school in Hunan's provincial capital at age seventeen. At the secondary school in Changsha, Mao faced a new set of challenges. Mocked and bullied for his peasant background, he was also ridiculed by wealthier students for his ragged clothes and different dialect. Again, it would be simple to read too much into such treatment. Taunting and bullying are all too common in every culture. Mean kids are everywhere. They do not explain the murderous lengths Mao Zedong would go to in creating a rigid Communist police state that permitted no dissent.

In addition to the bullying he encountered, Mao could also

sense a spirit of rebellion in Changsha. Young Mao realized there were changes in the air. One of the world's oldest civilizations was about to meet the modern world head-on.

During its many centuries of dynastic rule, China had become one of the most advanced civilizations on earth. The Chinese had invented gunpowder, paper, and the magnetic compass. It had been, as historian Daniel Boorstin once described it, "an empire without wants." That is one reason China had rejected most Western overtures. When King George III—the British king during the American Revolution— attempted to open trade with China, the emperor dismissed the request, saying, "There is nothing we lack." China, said the emperor, had no need of "your country's manufactures." Largely dependent upon agriculture, however, China worked with a system that had not changed for centuries and lagged behind other world powers by the late nineteenth century.

China's old imperial order, already weakened by corruption and poverty, was about to unravel. By 1911, just as European and Russian dynasties were falling to modern times, China's ancient imperial system was under attack. Mao saw the old ways collapsing to a desire for democracy and revolution.

The modern industrial world was forcing its way into China. Western nations desired Chinese products and wanted to sell things to China, including opium imported into China by the British. Resentful of these foreigners and the influence of Christian missionaries spreading across China, conservatives in the Chinese government began to enlist a secret society to destroy the foreign influence. Foreigners called members of this society Boxers because they practiced ritual exercises that looked like shadowboxing. By June 1900, the Boxers were burning churches and foreign residences, and killing Chinese Christian converts. Before long, China's empress dowager ordered that all foreigners be killed. Seven nations, including the United States, sent twenty thousand troops to put down what they considered a rebellion, and they seized the capital in August, ending the fighting. After a year of negotiations, China agreed to make reparations to the foreign nations. The Boxer Rebellion became a symbol of the imperial government's weakness in fending off foreign influence and power.

As the twentieth century arrived, many Chinese were ready to welcome modern ideas. One idea was to embrace democracy and end China's ancient monarchy. The leading force behind the

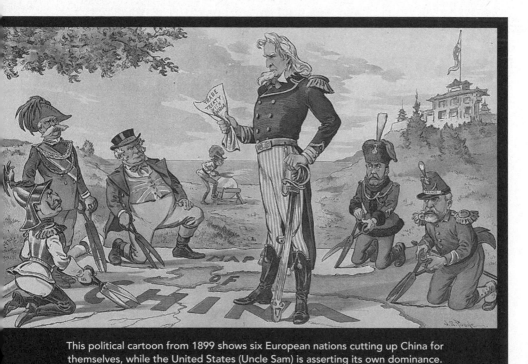

This political cartoon from 1899 shows six European nations cutting up China for themselves, while the United States (Uncle Sam) is asserting its own dominance.
[Wikimedia Commons]

emerging Chinese republican movement was a Western-educated Christian, Dr. Sun Yat-sen, who served as provisional president of a Chinese republic declared while the emperor still ruled. Sun Yat-sen is widely viewed as the man who threw off imperial rule and was considered the Father of His Country, much as George Washington was. Inspired by Sun Yat-sen's republican ideals, an army rose up, sparking a revolution in 1911. All across the sprawling country, local rebellions brought the ancient order down, sometimes with bloody massacres.

Dr. Sun Yat-sen in London in 1896.
[Wikimedia Commons]

Mao and some of his schoolmates joined the cause. To symbolize their rebellion against the emperor, Mao and his friends cut off their long pigtails. In every culture, hair has meaning beyond simple personal style. In China, the tradition of a long braided pigtail—or queue—was a centuries-old sign of subservience to the emperor. As newly shorn recruits in the rebellion, Mao and his friends never saw any action, but on February 12, 1912, the Chinese monarchy fell. China's last emperor, just six years old, abdicated the throne. And the Republic of China was created, bringing thousands of years of Chinese imperial rule to a sudden, crashing end. "Thinking the revolution was over, I resigned from the army and decided to return to my books," Mao Zedong said years later. "I had been a soldier for half a year."

Heading back to the classroom, Mao knew ancient traditions had been wiped away. Now he threw himself into reading such books as Adam Smith's *Wealth of Nations* and Montesquieu's *Spirit of Laws*, some of the most important books of philosophy behind modern free-market republics.

Contrary to Mao's belief that the revolution in China had come to an end, the Chinese republic of 1912 was short-lived and riven by turmoil. Rival factions across the vast country balked at a central government, and warring generals attempted to seize control of it.

By 1918, Mao was in his twenties and watching the chaos in his country and a world transformed by World War I. Russia had become a Communist state in 1917, with the promise of giving its land to peasants. Decisions in France that produced the Versailles Treaty in 1919 shaped

A teenage Mao Zedong with his pigtail gone, around 1913. [Wikimedia Commons]

events not only in Europe but also in faraway China. Even though China had been allied with the victors, the Versailles Treaty that ended the war gave Chinese territory once held by Germany to Japan. The news was met by waves of anger and violence in China toward the Japanese and the Western nations.

As the country seethed, Mao moved to Beijing. In the midst of the chaos of China's swirling politics and power grabs, he took a job as a librarian's assistant in the university. There he was introduced to the ideas of Karl Marx.

According to Marx, society was divided into classes of capitalists, laborers, and peasants. This division, Marx argued, was the fundamental source of injustice and inequality. He called for the laborers and peasants to join in a revolt, seize private property, and create a new society in which the workers shared land, business, and factories in common. All decisions would be made democratically and the wealth redistributed.

China was fertile territory for these Marxist ideas. In 1921, Mao and some friends gathered in a bookstore and voted to become a Communist group dedicated to the violent overthrow of the capitalist system. They joined others from around the country to form the Chinese Communist Party later that year. To begin their revolution, the Chinese Communists were willing to join forces with the Nationalists of Sun Yat-sen to end the reign of the warlords, even though the Nationalist goal for a democratic republic did not match the Communist vision. The alliance was even encouraged and supported by Stalin, who hoped to make China a new Soviet state.

During this period of alliance with the Nationalists, Mao

began to organize groups of peasant farmers and laborers. He understood that the millions of peasants could be a powerful political and military force.

The alliance with the Nationalists lasted six years.

After Sun Yat-sen's death in 1925, the Nationalists came under the control of General Chiang Kai-shek. Although Chiang's allegiances were unclear at first, he eventually broke with the Communists. He had the financial backing of Western powers fearful of a Communist takeover. They had seen the results of the Bolshevik Revolution in Russia and feared the bloodshed and end of private ownership that Bolshevism would bring to China. Chiang had a large army and vowed to wipe out the Communists.

When civil war broke out between the Nationalists and the Communists in 1927, Chiang proved to be a ruthless dictator in his own right, killing twenty thousand Communists within a few weeks of taking power. During decades of civil war, he was accused of starving and murdering any Chinese who might support the Communist cause.

General Chiang Kai-shek, leader of the Nationalist Chinese. [Wikimedia Commons]

Among the victims of the Nationalists was Mao's second wife, Yang Kaihui, the daughter of one of Mao's favorite teachers. They had married in 1920, and she bore three sons before they were separated by the turmoil. In 1930, she was captured and beheaded by a Nationalist general after she refused to renounce Mao and the Communist Party. Mao had by then married a third wife, He Zizhen, a devoted party member who would accompany Mao on the Long March, the expedition that would transform him into a living legend.

By 1931, Nationalist troops had chased the Communists into the countryside of southern China. In Jiangxi province the party established a base, and Mao continued organizing peasants and building the Red Army. But the Communists were disorganized and plagued by infighting. In October 1934, Chiang Kai-shek was close to delivering a fatal blow. Committing one million Nationalist soldiers, he planned to encircle and destroy the Red Army.

The Communist leadership ordered their eighty-six thousand soldiers to march, abandoning their base in Jiangxi carrying whatever they could. It was during this retreat that Mao, elected to a leadership position by the party, would secure his rise to power in the Chinese Communist Party.

If Mussolini's March on Rome was a calculated theatrical act, this march was an act of pure survival. Crisscrossing rivers and moving secretly, the marchers confused the Nationalists, who did not realize for three weeks that the Red Army had fled Jiangxi. Marching at night, carrying their weapons and supplies by horse cart and on men's backs, the Communists were making a desperate gamble. Crossing snowy mountains, with many marchers in summer clothing and wearing straw sandals, the march was treacherous and exhausting. When the enemy was not close by, a long column of torches could be seen snaking through valleys and over hills into the distance.

This was the beginning of the Long March, an event that would become a part of the foundational legend of Mao Zedong's Communist China. In China's Communist history, it achieved significance similar to George Washington's winter at Valley Forge—a combination of bravery and sheer endurance in the face of daunting odds and the force of nature. Lasting more than a year, the Long March covered some six thousand miles, subjecting thousands to starvation, aerial bombardment, and frequent skirmishes with Nationalist soldiers. The Red Army reached northern Shaanxi on October 20, 1935.

Only eight thousand or so of the eighty-six thousand who had set out completed the journey. Such losses might have signaled a major defeat. But the Red Army had crossed twenty-four rivers and eighteen mountain ranges, fighting Nationalists and warlords in some of China's most forbidding terrain every step of the way. It was turned into a great victory.

"The Long March is a manifesto," Mao said in a speech that December. "It has proclaimed to the world that the Red Army is an army of heroes, while the imperialists and their running dogs, Chiang Kai-shek and his like, are impotent. . . . The Long March is also a propaganda force. It has announced to some 200 million people in eleven provinces that the road of the Red Army is their only road to liberation."

The legend of Mao's exploits grew around China, and thousands of young Chinese began flocking to enlist in his Red Army. Mao Zedong, age forty-two, had emerged as the undisputed leader of the Chinese Communists.

As Mao and the Communists regrouped, China faced a new threat—the Japanese. With a call for a united front to fight their common foe, the civil war was suspended. In 1937, two years before World War II broke out in Europe, imperial Japan expanded its occupied territory in China. The Japanese had long exercised control of the province of Manchuria, but in 1937 Japan unleashed a new reign of terror. Widespread killings, rapes, and imprisonment in Nanking, Shanghai, and other major Chinese cities were all part of a brutal Japanese wartime occupation. Terrorized by the Japanese, hundreds of thousands of Chinese joined the Communist Red Army.

For the next eight years, the Communists fought the Japanese in a guerrilla war while Chiang Kai-shek pulled back from direct combat with Japan, hoping to preserve his forces. After the atomic bombs were dropped on Hiroshima and Nagasaki in August 1945, the Japanese surrendered to the United States, ending World War II. The Chinese civil war was on again. Still armed and supported by the United States and other Western nations, the Nationalists had more soldiers and better equipment than the Communists.

But Mao, who officially became chairman of the Chinese Communist Party in March 1943, had mystique and numbers on his side. The cult of personality surrounding him had already begun to emerge. In June 1937, the first picture of Mao was published, a print from a woodcut with his face illuminated by the rays of the sun, an image associated with China's past "emperor-worship." Since much of China was illiterate and rural, propaganda went beyond printed words. Posters with Mao's portrait appeared on buildings everywhere in Communist-controlled territory, and elementary school students were taught to chant, "We are all Chairman Mao's good little children." Loyalty to the party became strictly enforced discipline. Failure to go along meant public humiliation and trials in which party members denounced dissenters or resisters. A song, "The East Is Red," was composed as an anthem:

> **The East is Red, the sun rises.**
> **In China a Mao Zedong is born.**
> **He seeks the people's happiness.**
> **He is the people's Great Saviour.**

The phrase "Mao Zedong Thought" was coined and cemented into Chinese Communist propaganda. Many years later, another party leader would say, "Whatever accords with Mao Zedong Thought is right, while whatever does not accord with Mao Zedong Thought is wrong."

Propaganda as practiced by Mao's Communist Party was pervasive and effective. But Mao's most powerful weapon was the army of peasants at his command. From his mountain base in Shaanxi, Mao commanded more than nine hundred thousand soldiers. Using guerrilla war tactics, he and his generals wore down the Nationalist forces, which were weakened by widespread corruption in their ranks. In 1948, Mao and his generals mobilized one and a half million soldiers in what had been renamed the People's Liberation Army. With another two million peasant reserves, Mao and his generals finally forced Chiang Kai-shek to flee mainland China for the island of Taiwan off China's eastern coast, where the Republic of China was reestablished.

Through war, civil war, and political intrigues, Mao had prevailed. Appearing before a crowd of a hundred thousand people in Beijing's famous central Tiananmen Square on October 1, 1949, he stood in front of a two-story-high portrait of himself and proclaimed the People's Republic of China. Leading a one-party state, Mao and the Chinese Communists remade Chinese society, using all the tools of the Strongman: control of the media, violent elimination of any rivals or opposition, suppression of dissent, a secret police to enforce complete conformity to party rule, widespread propaganda, and control of the all-important army.

It was Mao's decision to send part of the People's Liberation Army to Korea in October 1950 to support North Korea in the Korean War. The United States was leading the fight to protect South Korea from Communist North Korea under the authority of the United Nations. It was a period of the Cold War between the United States and the Soviet Union and its Chinese ally when a much wider war seemed possible. A war with Mao's China and the use of atomic weapons were both considered as the war was fought to a stalemate and an eventual cease-fire in 1953 that left the Korean peninsula divided.

As the Chinese army fought in Korea, Mao opened up a "land reform" movement in which land was taken from landlords and given to poor peasants. During this period, estimates of the number of landlords and rural power-holders who died range from two hundred thousand to two million. During the same time, hundreds of thousands of businessmen, former Nationalists, professors, writers, and artists were accused of being "counterrevolutionaries" and beaten to death at mass meetings or otherwise executed.

Mao and Jiang Qing, his fourth wife, later known as Madame Mao.
[Wikimedia Commons]

Mao had established complete control over the party and the country. That complete control was clear in Mao's announcement of the Great Leap Forward, an attempt to transform China into an economic power. Like Stalin's campaigns in the Soviet Union and Ukraine, policies to increase industrial production in China backfired, leading to one of the worst famines in history. An estimated twenty to forty million people died between 1959 and 1962. Some resorted to cannibalism, others to suicide.

"Mao, the Great Helmsman, promised in 1958 that China would catch up to the West in fifteen years," writes author Gordon Chang. "Mao's utopian mass campaign to decentralize industrialization to backyard furnaces and collectivize agriculture into communes ended in the deaths of tens of millions of people. . . . Bodies literally littered the fields, but few were willing to tell Party leaders that the people were suffering from their ill-conceived policies."

Mao and party leaders placed blame elsewhere—on foreigners, reactionaries, counterrevolutionaries, and dissidents. While quietly making changes to his disastrous plan, Mao withdrew from his highly visible position to escape plots being made against him. When he learned that he was being secretly tape-recorded by other party members seeking his removal, Mao responded brutally to the threat. In 1966, he called for the Cultural Revolution to reestablish his unquestioned control.

"Cultural Revolution" was a label for Mao's claim that elements in the government were trying to restore capitalism. Calling for violent "class struggle," he unleashed millions of young people in the Red Guards. These fanatical young people had been

Mao Zedong in 1963.
[Wikimedia Commons]

reared on the cult of Maoism. Indoctrinated, or brainwashed, since birth, they were devoted to their Great Helmsman and did as they were told.

In August 1966, one million Red Guards converged on Beijing's central Tiananmen Square. Detachments of school-children and college students, singing revolutionary songs and carrying red silk banners and portraits of the chairman, began marching down the Avenue of Eternal Peace to take up their positions. "Mao's appearance was timed to coincide with the first rays of the rising sun," writes biographer Philip Short. "An orgasm of devotional enthusiasm swept feverishly through the streets. A few independent spirits saw through the divine cha-rade, like the student who wrote a few weeks later: 'The Great Cultural Revolution is not a mass movement, but one man moving the masses with the barrel of a gun.'"

And that one man was able to unleash the furies of his peo-ple. Like all Strongmen, Mao employed mass propaganda. It had shaped China for decades, directing the students to stamp out old ideas, culture, and customs. They were told to elimi-nate the threats to the revolution—described as "landlords, rich peasants, counter-revolutionaries, bad elements and Rightists." The party would define exactly who posed such threats, and they would be dealt with harshly.

The fourth and last of Mao's wives was Jiang Qing, who married Mao in 1938 after he was granted a divorce from He Zizhen. Known later as "Madame Mao," Jiang was in charge of much of the propaganda behind the Cultural Revolution as part of a group known as the Gang of Four. (After Mao's death, she and the other three officials were ousted from government and tried for their acts during the Cultural Revolution. Jiang was sentenced to death, which was later commuted to life imprisonment. She reportedly died by suicide in May 1991.)

A whirlwind had been unleashed. Under orders from party leaders, the Red Guards tortured, looted, and killed as they saw fit. Teachers and "stinking intellectuals" were especially targeted, and there are gruesome accounts of teachers being shot, buried alive, or forced to sit on explosives and light them.

A form of nationwide madness followed. In the violent struggle that swept across China, millions of people were persecuted and suffered public humiliation, imprisonment, torture, hard labor, seizure of property, and executions. A large segment of the population, including young people from the cities, was forced to move to the countryside to labor for the party. Whatever individual will that might have existed was crushed in conformity to the party line.

In a memoir of the period, Moying Li describes an incident from when she was twelve years old. The Red Guards had come to her school and pushed a headmaster onto a stage in front of the schoolchildren. He was kicked and forced to kneel. The man's daughter was brought onstage and told to denounce her father. In tears, the seven-year-old could barely speak. "Chairman Mao's children never shed tears," a Red Guard leader told her. "You said you love Chairman Mao, right?" The girl nodded and then was forced to beat her father with a stick.

Through it all, Mao wielded the levers of violence and power. "He was cold and calculating, but also erratic, whimsical, and fitful, thriving in willed chaos," writes Frank Dikötter in a history of the period. "He improvised, bending and breaking millions along the way. He may not have been in control, but he was always in charge, relishing a game in which he could constantly rewrite the rules."

A child during the Cultural Revolution, Chinese writer Da Chen, a distinguished author who passed away in December 2019, remembers the Red Guards parading by his house carrying rifles, and shouting revolutionary slogans. His father was fired from his teaching job for disloyalty, and the family had been stripped of all property owned by his grandfather, a landlord. For months, Da Chen had nothing to eat but tree bark and wild roots. "One year, we ate moldy yams three times a day for four months," Da Chen recalled. "Most of the time Dad was away at labor camp, or Grandpa was being detained in the commune jail, waiting for another public humiliation meeting in the market square, where he would be beaten badly." In secret, he prayed to the hidden Buddha in his house—concealed because religion was illegal in Communist China. "I asked for Dad not to get beaten by the Red Guards, for Grandpa to be well, for

Mom not to cry as much," wrote Da Chen. "My last request was always for food—more of it, please."

Religion—whether Buddhism, Christianity, Islam, or any other faith—had been replaced by the worship of Mao. His signature tunic, the Mao jacket, became the uniform of the people. Besides uniformity in dress, uniformity in thought was demanded. Everyone was expected to wear the same thing, to look alike, to think alike. To express any individuality during the Cultural Revolution carried a heavy price.

Like clothing, reading was strictly dictated. Of course, books change people and shape cultures. Mao understood this. That is why, for decades, every Chinese citizen was expected to own *Quotations from Chairman Mao*, also known as the Little Red Book. They had to carry it, memorize it, and repeat its teachings in public meetings. To this day, more than a billion copies have been published, making the book, often wrapped in its distinctive red vinyl cover, one of the most widely produced of all time. Mao's picture appeared on the front page of the state-run *People's Daily* often, accompanied by quotations from the Little Red Book.

Originally produced in 1964 by the People's Liberation Army, the book soon became central to the leader's personality cult as well as a bible of thought control. Everything George Orwell imagined in his novel *1984* actually happened in China. The Orwellian-sounding Ministry of Culture aimed to distribute a copy of Mao's book to every Chinese citizen. Mao reportedly liked its resemblance to books of quotations by philosophers such as Confucius. Among its many tenets, was this "wisdom":

Carrying tasseled spears, a group of Chinese schoolchildren wearing Red Guard armbands chant as they parade through the streets of Harbin in October 1966 during the Cultural Revolution. [Li Zhensheng/Contact Press Images]

☆ "We must have faith in the masses and we must have faith in the Party. These are two cardinal principles. If we doubt these principles, we shall accomplish nothing."

☆ "A revolution is not a dinner party, or writing an essay, or painting a picture, or doing embroidery; it cannot be so refined, so leisurely and gentle, so temperate, kind, courteous, restrained and magnanimous. A revolution is an insurrection, an act of violence by which one class overthrows another."

☆ **"We should support whatever the enemy opposes and oppose whatever the enemy supports."**

☆ **"Every Communist must grasp the truth, 'Political power grows out of the barrel of a gun.'"**

The active phase of the Cultural Revolution continued through 1971, the year of the Ping-Pong diplomacy that changed China and the world. But the upheaval carried over until 1976, the year of Mao's death. Having suffered a stroke and also having been diagnosed with Parkinson's disease and cancer, Mao was in his final days. He had a series of heart attacks on September 9, 1976, and he died at the age of eighty-two. But the impact of the Cultural Revolution continued in China's politics up until Mao's death and even past it.

Years after his death, some of Mao's legendary glow began to wear off, especially for Westerners unfamiliar with Chinese ways. Celebrated as a farm boy and man of the people, the Great Helmsman was depicted as a man who had never given up many of his rural Chinese ways. He was said to have had no use for Western-style plumbing; when he was the supreme leader of millions of Chinese, one of his bodyguards was assigned to dig an outdoor latrine as a bathroom. His personal physician for more than twenty years also revealed that Mao refused to be treated for a sexually transmitted disease, though he knew he was spreading it to the young women who shared his bed.

Today the corpse of the Great Helmsman still lies in a place of honor: the grandiose Chairman Mao Memorial Hall in the center of Tiananmen Square, a granite mausoleum that is the symbolic center of this nation of more than 1.3 billion. Every year, hundreds of thousands of people stand in line, sometimes for hours, to view for a few seconds the embalmed body of the man so many Chinese still revere. He was the same man who was responsible for so many deaths in the Great Leap Forward and then began the Cultural Revolution. Despite those costs and other atrocities committed by many in his name, Mao left a complicated legacy for China—much as Stalin did for the Soviet Union. Both men united their countries and brought them into the twentieth century. They turned nations of poor farmers into modern industrial powers with atomic bombs and space programs.

The extraordinary meeting with Richard Nixon, which came near the end of Mao's life, launched China on a path of loosening control. Private property was restored, international business and investment was eventually welcomed, and the result today is a China that is a far cry from any that the son of a farmer in Hunan could have imagined—a land of high-tech billionaires, aspiring young entrepreneurs, and a generation of Chinese students who study all over the world.

In the years since that exchange with Nixon, China has emerged as the world's second-largest economy, after the United States. Its transformation has been powered by a profound change in its economy. In 2013, China's leaders described the new "Chinese Dream": national rejuvenation, improvement of people's livelihoods, prosperity, construction of a better society, and military strength—which they claim can all be best achieved under one-party, Socialist rule.

Modern Chinese leaders maintain the powerful and iconic image of Chairman Mao as the Great Helmsman and the Father of His Country. They believe that he is a symbol of national pride. Since Mao's death, nationalism "has provided the glue to hold the country together in an era when ideology has lost its appeal," biographer Philip Short writes. "These three pillars—prosperity, nationalism, and the legend of Mao's revolution—are the foundations on which Chinese political power is based."

Legends are powerful.

TIME LINE—
THE LIFE OF SADDAM HUSSEIN

April 28, 1937 ··· Saddam Hussein is born near Tikrit, on the Tigris River in northwestern Iraq.

July 14, 1958 ··· The Iraqi monarchy is overthrown in a coup.

July 30, 1968 ··· Saddam's Baath Party takes power in a coup.

June 1979 ··· Saddam becomes president of Iraq.

Sept. 23, 1980 ··· The Iran-Iraq War begins; an estimated 500,000 Iraqi and Iranian soldiers die in the conflict.

March 1988 ··· Saddam uses poison gas against the minority Kurds in Iraq.

Aug. 1988 ··· A cease-fire is declared in the war.

Aug. 2, 1990 ··· Iraq invades neighboring Kuwait.

Jan. 16–Feb. 28, 1991 ··· Gulf War: With United Nations approval, a coalition of thirty-nine nations, led by the United States, forces Iraq out of Kuwait.

Sept. 11, 2001 ··· Terrorists associated with al-Qaeda leader Osama bin Laden attack the World Trade Center.

Mar. 20, 2003 ··· President George W. Bush announces an invasion of Iraq to topple Saddam Hussein.

Dec. 13, 2003 ··· U.S. forces capture Saddam Hussein.

Dec. 30, 2006 ··· Convicted of crimes against humanity by an Iraqi court, Saddam Hussein is executed by hanging.

STALIN ON THE TIGRIS

U.S. troops enter Baghdad under the "Hands of Victory." [Wikimedia Commons]

THE STORY
OF
SADDAM HUSSEIN

The great duel, the mother of all battles has begun. . . .
The dawn of victory nears as this great showdown begins.

—Saddam Hussein

• • •

Mr. Hussein held on to the ethos of a village peasant who
believed that the strongman was everything.

—Saddam's obituary, *New York Times*

• • •

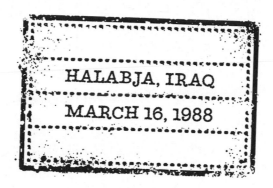

ON A MARCH MORNING in 1988, warplanes flew over Halabja, a town in northern Iraq near the border with Iran. That was not unusual. There was a war going on between the two countries.

But these planes were close enough to the ground that witnesses could see their markings. They were flown by the Iraqi air force. And then bombs dropped by Iraqi planes fell on the Iraqi town.

"It was different from the other bombs," said a witness. "There was a huge sound, a huge flame, and it had very destructive ability. If you touched one part of your body that had been burned, your hand burned also. It caused things to catch fire."

The burning sensation was only the beginning. When people emerged from their makeshift bomb shelters, they saw friends and family dead, frozen in grotesque positions. For some, death had been instantaneous. For others, it came slowly. When reports of the attack emerged, Iraq blamed Iran. But the truth was soon clear. The Iraqi regime led by Strongman

Saddam Hussein had attacked the Kurds living in Iraq with illegal chemical weapons.

In the final months of an eight-year war between Iraq and Iran, ethnic Kurdish fighters who sided with Iran had moved into Halabja in the Kurdistan region of Iraq near the border with Iran. The large farming town was home to more than forty thousand people, mostly Kurds. An ethnic group without a state of their own, the Kurds had been spread out over parts of Iraq, Iran, Syria, and Turkey. Most who fell victim to the chemical weapons were Kurdish civilians, not fighters, who were caught in the cross fire in the long struggle between two warring oil powers.

"Halabja quickly became known as the Kurdish Hiroshima," writes Pulitzer Prize–winning author Samantha Power. "In three days of attacks, victims were exposed to mustard gas, which burns, mutates DNA, and causes malformations and cancer; and the nerve gases sarin and tabun, which can kill, paralyze, or cause immediate and lasting neuropsychiatric damage. Doctors suspect that the dreaded VX gas and the biological agent aflatoxin were also employed. Some 5,000 Kurds were killed immediately."

The deadly gas attack on Halabja's Kurds was part of a brutal war that started in 1980, when Saddam Hussein launched an attack on neighboring Iran, hoping to take advantage of the chaos following the overthrow of its leader, the shah, the year before. But Saddam miscalculated. Led by the Ayatollah Khomeini (a Muslim cleric), the Iranian military and Iran's people rallied to their country's defense. In the punishing war that followed, a half million men on both sides were killed.

Saddam's use of poison gas on his own people came as no surprise to many observers. They had witnessed his rise to power and knew that he modeled himself on Joseph Stalin and his murderous regime.

The son of peasants, Saddam Hussein was born in 1937, in a mud hut on stilts in a village near Tikrit, in northern Iraq, one of the poorest regions in the country. There are varying stories of Saddam's childhood, so it is not clear whether Saddam's father deserted his mother or died of cancer before he was born. One fact is certain: Saddam grew up in crushing poverty and had little education. Saddam's mother, Sabha, abandoned him at an early age, and he went to live with his uncle, Khairallah Talfah, an army officer in nearby Tikrit.

At the time, Iraq was a recently created, independent nation ruled by a monarch, but Great Britain still had widespread influence in the country. Carved out of the old Ottoman Empire and made part of the British Empire after the First World War, Iraq stands as another example of the ghosts of Versailles haunting the world. So do the Kurds, whose territory was divided up by Europeans after the war.

Saddam's uncle had fought against the British and had been jailed for his nationalist activities. In his uncle's house, Saddam learned to hate the British, the Jews, and the "Persians" (Iraqi Shiites and Iranians; Saddam and his family were Sunni, a rival branch of Islam). Khairallah Talfah steeped his nephew in stories of Arab heroes such as Saladin, a Kurdish Muslim born in Tikrit who expelled the Christian Crusaders from Jerusalem in

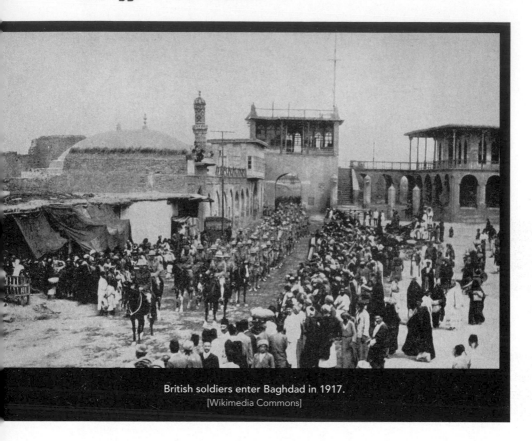

British soldiers enter Baghdad in 1917.
[Wikimedia Commons]

1187. Just as Mussolini had visions of ancient Rome's glories, Saddam Hussein envisioned an Iraqi future tied to a glorious ancient imperial era, when Babylon was the "cradle of civilization" with a reputation for great splendor.

Khairallah Talfah also tutored young Saddam in the world view of the Baath Party, a political group that mixed Arab nationalism, Socialism, and militant anti-Western sentiments. (*Ba'ath* is Arabic for "renaissance.") After joining the group, Saddam assassinated a rival in Tikrit. In 1958, the pro-Western king of Iraq and the prime minister were assassinated in a coup. A year later, the Baath Party selected twenty-two-year-old Saddam to be part of a hit squad to take out the coup's leader, who had become Iraq's prime minister. The attempt failed, but a wounded Saddam escaped, making his way to Syria and then Egypt in fear for his life.

After a military coup brought the Baath Party to power, Saddam was able to safely return to Iraq, and in 1963, he married his uncle's daughter (his first cousin). The Baathist regime was overthrown after nine months, however, and the party didn't regain power until July 1968. By that time, Saddam had risen to assistant secretary-general of the party, and was instrumental in the coup that brought his party to power once again. He would take charge of internal security and was responsible for the executions of seventeen people accused of being spies for Israel in January 1969. After this public hanging, *New York Times* reporter Neil MacFarquhar wrote, "Hundreds of arrests and executions followed as the civilian wing of the Baath Party gradually eclipsed the Iraqi military."

By November 1969, Saddam had eliminated many rivals and dissidents. Having gained more power, he molded a secret police force and, like his Strongman predecessors, began to master the brutal business of suppressing enemies, rivals, and dissenters.

"The [Baath Party] developed the politics of fear into an art form, one that ultimately served the purpose of legitimizing their rule by making large numbers of people complicit in the violence of the regime. . . . At the apex of the system of punishment sat torture," writes Kanan Makiya in his history of Iraq under Saddam, *Republic of Fear* (first published under a pseudonym).

In 1981, the international human rights organization Amnesty International reported, "The various forms of torture included the beating of bare feet with a rubber truncheon, 'systematic electric shock torture,' burnings, mock executions, sexual abuse, and physical assaults with fists, boots, sticks and whips."

Eventually Saddam took complete control of the party and country when the ailing Baath leader was forced from power in 1979. Quickly demonstrating his Stalin-inspired techniques, Saddam executed a group of rivals in a violent purge reminiscent of Hitler's Night of the Long Knives or Stalin's Great Terror.

One party official was tortured and threatened with his family's execution until he "confessed" to a made-up plot against the Iraqi government. At a Baath Party gathering, this official's supposed co-conspirators were removed from the room one by one as Saddam called their names. "Guards dragged away each of the accused," according to the *New York Times*. "Mr. Hussein paused from reading occasionally to light his cigar, while the room erupted in almost hysterical chanting demanding death to traitors. The entire dark spectacle, designed to leave no doubt as to who controlled Iraq, was filmed and copies distributed around the country." More than twenty men were executed by firing squads.

"Saddam Hussein borrowed from Stalinism," reveals Saïd K. Aburish, a man who once worked in Saddam's government. "He had his security people trained in Eastern Europe, particularly East Germany. Then he brought them back to Iraq and

he taught them how to use the tribal linkage to eliminate people. So whereas they used Stalinist methods to discover people
who were opposed to the regime, after that came the tribal fac-
tor, when Saddam said 'Don't get rid of Abdullah, get rid of his
whole family, because one member of his family might assassi-
nate us.' And that made it a perfect system for Iraq."

Under any dictatorship, there is always a "carrot or the
stick" bargain, with life and death hanging in the balance. The
Strongman dangles the carrot of power and wealth before
those who prove their loyalty and take part in his cruelty. For
those who refuse, resist, or challenge the Strongman, he brings
the stick—torture, imprisonment, and death.

Such a bargain erases any potential opponents and ensures
the loyalty of followers. But Saddam also had learned another
key lesson in the Strongman's playbook. Iraq is home to a great
abundance of oil reserves, and as the nation's oil riches grew,
he launched massive public work programs, including the construction of numerous personal palaces. It was a strategy that
had worked in Germany, where Adolf Hitler had won early
praise for ending mass unemployment by rebuilding German
cities and creating Germany's high-speed autobahns. In Iraq,
Saddam brought electricity to rural villages and built modern
highways.

These building projects served another specific purpose—
extending Saddam's cult of personality. Everywhere Iraqis
looked, they saw concrete reminders of their nation's leader.
Mosques, airports, neighborhoods, and entire cities were built
and then named after Saddam. A military arch erected in

Baghdad in 1989 was said to be modeled on his forearms and then enlarged forty times to hold two giant crossed swords.

"While Mr. Hussein was in power, his statue guarded the entrance to every village, his portrait watched over each government office and he peered down from at least one wall in every home," writes *New York Times* correspondent Neil MacFarquhar. "His picture was so widespread that a joke quietly circulating among his detractors in 1988 put the country's population at 34 million — 17 million people and 17 million portraits of Saddam."

This is all part of what goes into building a cult of personality around a dictator. Through massive construction projects

Baghdad's Victory Arch. [Wikimedia Commons]

and propaganda, the man becomes larger than life in the eyes of the people. He impresses those who admire such a leader, even as he builds gilded palaces for himself, while those who protest or fail to show sufficient enthusiasm are always at risk.

"Mr. Hussein held on to the ethos of a village peasant who believed that the strongman was everything," says MacFarquhar.

Like Mussolini's Italy, Hitler's Germany, the Soviet Union of Stalin, and Mao's China, Iraq quickly became a "party state." Baath membership was mandatory for the educated and ambitious. Special Republican Guards, drawn from the Sunni tribes beholden to Saddam, provided an elite, highly trained, and well-armed personal army. Skimming vast sums from the oil dollars that flowed into Iraq, Saddam Hussein showered immense wealth on himself and his favored supporters, usually members of his extended clan. As in all of the Strongman stories, the secret police enforced Saddam's will everywhere. Fear was pervasive. And torture, or the threat of torture, was the glue holding the regime in power.

Eventually in Saddam's Iraq, torture of political prisoners, "criminals," and army deserters became standard policy. According to Amnesty International in a 2001 report, the brutality was bone chilling: the loss of an ear for desertion; eyes, tongues, and toenails removed to prompt forced confessions by those interrogated by his security services. "Victims have described to Amnesty International how they have been beaten with canes, whips, hosepipe or metal rods and how they have been suspended for hours from either a rotating fan in the ceiling or from a horizontal pole often in contorted positions as electric shocks were applied repeatedly on their bodies. Some victims had been forced to watch others, including their own relatives or family members, being tortured in front of them."

Fear of being punished for any dissent, a hint of opposition— or sometimes for no real reason—hung over Iraq's people like a foreboding cloud. Many accounts of sadistic torture and relentless violence under Saddam emerged clearly after 2003, when Iraq was invaded by the United States. According to an account in the *Boston Globe*, the victims included former political prisoners, relatives of the executed, and other "enemies of the state" who lost an arm, an ear, or a foot to the torturer's knife.

Saddam's personal doctor recounted his own imprisonment: "For the first five years, he put me in a cell by myself, 2 meters by 2½ meters, where I didn't know if it was day or night. I was so dirty with lice. There were cockroaches in my mouth at night. And they came to beat you in the morning and at night for nothing, nothing."

The words "for nothing, nothing" recall the grim passage in George Orwell's *1984*: "Power is not a means; it is an end. One does not establish a dictatorship in order to safeguard a revolution; one makes the revolution in order to establish the dictatorship. The object of persecution is persecution. The object of torture is torture. The object of power is power."

Like other Strongmen, Saddam Hussein also wanted to build the allegiance of young people. Many young Iraqis, especially the poor, were recruited into youth groups called Saddam's Lion

Cubs, whose aims were indoctrination and loyalty to Saddam and the Baath Party. At "summer camps," one boy remembered long marches in oppressive heat, being slapped by military trainers for not following orders, and spending nights in fields listening to the howls of wolves. The camps culminated each August with a ceremony in which the youths were videotaped in the Iraqi fighter tradition of ripping a dog's flesh with their teeth.

"The dogs were already dead," said a young man who was thirteen when he attended the camp in 1998. He still recalled the bitter taste. "It was horrible."

A form of hellish sadism was the prominent feature of another of Saddam's dreams. He wanted to build Iraq into a sports power and launch a world-class Olympic soccer team. Saddam placed control of Iraq's Olympic Committee in the hands of his older son, Uday. By many accounts, Uday Hussein surpassed his father's cruelty, turning Olympic training into a terrifying exercise in shame and torture.

Under Uday, athletes' heads were shaved to humiliate them if they failed on the field or did not train hard enough. Some were hung upside down and had the soles of their feet whipped. Others were buried in hot sand up to their necks. Fingers or ears were amputated, and electric shocks were applied to their skin. In the case of soccer players, they were forced to kick concrete balls.

Immanuel Baba Dano, coach of the national soccer team, recalled how athletes were smeared with feces and jailed. Others suffocated in a sarcophagus with nails pointed inward to puncture them, he said. Wild dogs tore a few players to pieces. It's still not clear how many athletes were killed.

Uday also kept two lions caged on a farm. When two university students were arrested on his orders, they were taken to the farm. Uday's former executioner told the *Sunday Times* of London in 2003 that the young men were fed to the lions.

"We knew Saddam was tough," says Saïd K. Aburish, who worked for Saddam. "He was also delivering. The Iraqi people were getting a great deal of things that they needed and wanted and he was popular. He eliminated people here and there. With time, as with all dictators, the balance switched. And all we saw of Saddam was elimination and very little benefit to the people."

In some ways, according to dissidents and others who escaped, the entire country had become a torture camp in which loyalty and order were maintained by fear. With a grandiose vision of himself as leader of the Arab world, Saddam paid cash to journalists to turn out admiring articles about him. He also funded terrorists and pressed Iraq's scientists and engineers to produce weapons of mass destruction, including chemical weapons—like those he used on the Kurds—and a possible atomic bomb or other radioactive weapons.

For this, he needed more oil money. "Oil, money, arms, terror," writes Harvey Sicherman, "these were the tools of the would-be Stalin on the Tigris."

Saddam's strike at Iran's oil fields had led to the disastrous eight-year war for both countries. A mere two years after that war ended, he struck again in August 1990, when he invaded

Kuwait, another oil-rich neighbor that bordered even wealthier Saudi Arabia. Kuwait was virtually defenseless and much smaller than Iran. But Kuwait had powerful friends.

Saddam Hussein's invasion led to another disaster for Iraq. Mobilizing the United Nations against Saddam was U.S. president George Herbert Walker Bush. He was the first Bush president, father of George W. Bush. Moving quickly to counter Iraq, the elder Bush established Operation Desert Shield to protect the vast oil fields of nearby Saudi Arabia. He understood that a quick strike by Saddam's forces into the Saudi kingdom would put control of more than 40 percent of the world's oil reserves in Saddam's hands. Such an incredibly important resource in the hands of a Strongman was a frightening prospect, particularly given Saddam's willingness to emulate his role model, Joseph Stalin. Although there was considerable U.S. rhetoric that this was a war to defend freedom, both Kuwait and Saudi Arabia were feudal monarchies with little interest in human rights or democratic liberties, so it would seem the true motive was blocking Saddam's effort to control a vast reserve of the world's oil.

With United Nations approval, the United States next spearheaded a coalition of thirty-nine nations to push Iraq out of Kuwait. In Operation Desert Storm, days of devastating air strikes were followed by a swift, decisive ground offensive. The conflict, which Saddam had boasted would be "the mother of all battles," lasted just forty-two days. As the U.S.-led coalition routed his army, the Iraqi Strongman ordered Kuwait's oil wells to be set on fire. He wanted to destroy them as well as provide cover for his troops from air strikes. The fires were eventually contained, and Kuwait was soon liberated.

Saddam Hussein might have been toppled at that moment. But the U.S.-led offensive was halted because President Bush and his advisers said they had fulfilled the United Nations' terms of the action against Iraq. Bush and his national security advisor, Brent Scowcroft, later wrote in their 1998 book, *A World Transformed*, "Had we gone the invasion route, the United States could conceivably still be an occupying power in a bitterly hostile land. It would have been a dramatically different—and perhaps barren—outcome."

Saddam's ability to strike his neighbors had been crippled, and Iraq was devastated. Tens of thousands of Iraqi soldiers and thousands of civilians were killed. Violent uprisings broke out against Saddam's regime among the Kurds and in other regions. But instead of being weakened, Saddam seemed to tighten his grip. Iraqi troops put down most of the rebellions with brutal efficiency that relied once again on mass murder, torture, rape, and indiscriminate killing by the military. "The rebel fighters retreated into the mountains with their families," recorded Dave Johns. "As they backed away, Iraqi helicopters threw flour on them . . . a cruel reminder of the powdery chemical weapons that killed Kurds by the thousands."

For the next ten years, Saddam continued his terror state.

Then on September 11, 2001, the terrorist group al-Qaeda attacked the World Trade Center in New York City and the Pentagon in Washington, D.C. The United States responded with an invasion of Afghanistan in order to topple the Taliban, the fundamentalist Sunni Islamic group that had controlled that country since 1996 and had allowed al-Qaeda's leader, Osama bin Laden, to plot the 9/11 attacks.

Although there was no evidence that Iraq had been involved in the 9/11 attacks, Saddam was America's next target. George W. Bush—the younger President Bush—demanded that Iraq eliminate its weapons of mass destruction, refrain from supporting terrorism, and end the repression of its people. These became the officially stated reasons for going to war in Iraq—the first preemptive war in American history—to achieve "regime change," that is, to eliminate Saddam Hussein as Iraq's leader. However, the claims of the Bush administration that Saddam had links with al-Qaeda were not credible, and the belief that Iraq was on the verge of acquiring nuclear weapons and other weapons of mass destruction was quickly refuted after his regime fell.

Baghdad and much of Iraq were soon overwhelmed by American air power—a campaign famously described as one of "shock and awe," which played out on televisions like a deadly video game. Less than six weeks after launching the assault, American troops had landed and were in nominal control of Baghdad. Iraq's military forces either were destroyed, had surrendered, or had gone into hiding. Saddam and his two sons also disappeared.

Offering millions of dollars for information on the whereabouts of Saddam and his closest advisers, the United States began an intense manhunt across the defeated country. The bounty prompted a tip about Saddam's sons, Uday and Qusay, who, many believe, were being groomed to fill his shoes one day. On July 22, 2003, they were killed in a shootout when U.S. soldiers raided a villa in Mosul, in northern Iraq.

On December 13, 2003, U.S. soldiers found Saddam Hussein hiding in an eight-foot-deep hole, not far from his birthplace near Tikrit.

After a trial, Saddam Hussein was sentenced to death. He was executed by hanging on December 30, 2006, a little more than three years after his capture.

When Saddam's regime fell, the world got a better view of the terror that had gripped Iraq under his reign. "The objects unearthed at Iraqi prisons, palaces and safe houses speak

An Iraqi-American translator with U.S. Special Forces pins Saddam Hussein to the ground at the time of his capture in December 2003. [Wikimedia Commons]

of brutality and indulgence," reported the *New York Times* in May 2003. "A gold machine gun. A cable used to deliver electric shocks to ears and genitals. Fantasy paintings of snakes, monsters and unclad women. A red wire cage with a cement channel in the floor for human excrement."

Abu Ghraib, about twenty miles from Baghdad, was one of those prisons. In Saddam's era, Abu Ghraib "was one of the world's most notorious prisons, with torture, weekly executions, and vile living conditions," writes Pulitzer Prize–winning investigative journalist Seymour Hersh. "As many as fifty thousand men and women—no accurate count is possible—were jammed into Abu Ghraib at one time, in twelve-by-twelve-foot cells that were little more than human holding pits."

The complex was cleaned and repaired by the occupying U.S. Army and converted into a military prison. Under U.S. control, however, Abu Ghraib reverted to its former notoriety, as U.S. soldiers and other officials in U.S. intelligence agencies were accused of widespread mistreatment of Iraqi prisoners in Saddam's former torture palace. Army and congressional investigations followed and revealed a frightful record of abuses.

"Army regulations and the Geneva conventions were routinely violated, and . . . much of the day-to-day management of the prisoners was abdicated to Army military-intelligence units and civilian contract employees," Hersh reported. "Interrogating prisoners and getting intelligence, including by intimidation and torture, was the priority."

No nation has a monopoly on vice or virtue. The crimes committed by Americans in that place are a grim reminder of how short the path to brutality can be. Saddam's former torture hellhole was a place whose origins must be tied back to his great inspiration, Joseph Stalin.

"He had an entire room of one palace dedicated to Stalin: pictures, books and memorabilia from and about the dictator," said Mary Habeck, a Yale University history professor. "Like Stalin, he won the hearts of the poor and dispossessed by pushing literacy and education and opening up job opportunities. Like Stalin, he then carried out a coup that left him alone at the top with the complete loyalty of the bureaucracy, army and secret police. Like Stalin, he punished any hint of dissent with the utmost severity. And like Stalin, he put thousands of informers and enforcers amongst his people to keep them in line."

In Shakespeare's *Julius Caesar*, a play about one of history's most famous Strongmen, the character Mark Anthony says, "The evil that men do lives after them; the good is oft interred with their bones."

Mussolini, Hitler, Stalin, Mao, Saddam Hussein. It is difficult to find the good that was buried with them, but the evil has certainly lived after them. Can their evil ways be explained? Is there some Strongman syndrome that identifies such brutal killers? Are they simply insane madmen? Many historians have weighed in on that question.

"Like Stalin and Hitler, Mr. Hussein has sometimes been referred to as a madman, in part because people are reluctant to accept such ruthlessness and cruelty as the product of anything but insanity," Erica Goode wrote after Saddam Hussein's capture in 2003. "But bad does not equal mad. Most historical analysts have rejected the notion that mental illness could explain the actions of either Stalin or Hitler." She adds that experts familiar with Saddam's upbringing and years in power said that there was no evidence that he suffered from psychosis or any severe mental illness.

Other researchers, explains Goode, believe that Saddam was more accurately described as a "malignant narcissist." The term describes a mix of personality traits: sadism, aggression, paranoia, and antisocial behavior combined with an extreme sense of self-grandeur. It has been applied to Stalin and Hitler. These type of leaders share four qualities, according to Dr. Jerrold M. Post, an expert in political psychology: extreme self-absorption, paranoia, no constraints of conscience, and a willingness to use whatever means necessary to accomplish goals.

Saddam Hussein had shown over many years, and at terrible costs in lives and the fate of Iraqis, that he was willing to use any means necessary. In assessing Saddam Hussein, Erica Goode concluded he was a man "who acted out his fantasies of omnipotence using a nation as his theater and its citizens as his props."

NEVER AGAIN?

The Lincoln
Memorial.
[Wikimedia
Commons]

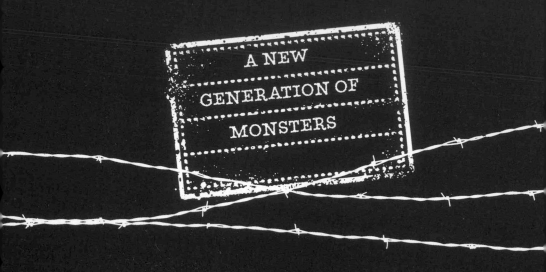

A NEW GENERATION OF MONSTERS

As I would not be a *slave*, so I would not be a master.
This expresses my idea of democracy. Whatever differs
from this, to the extent of the difference, is no democracy.

—Abraham Lincoln

• • •

For those denounced by their smug, horrible children
For a peppermint-star and the praise of the Perfect State,
For all those strangled, gelded or merely starved
To make perfect states; for the priest hanged in his cassock,
The Jew with his chest crushed in and his eyes dying,
The revolutionist lynched by the private guards
To make perfect states, in the names of the perfect states.

—Stephen Vincent Benét, "Litany for Dictatorships"

• • •

All animals are equal but some animals
are more equal than others.

—George Orwell, *Animal Farm*

• • •

"NEVER AGAIN" and "Lest we forget" are simple slogans, easily remembered and frequently repeated. But have they done the world any good?

Some of the terrible events outlined in this book are hideously gruesome chapters from fairly recent world history. They keep repeating. The suffering sometimes seems to be an endless loop.

World leaders, historians, teachers, and many others speak frequently about the atrocities and tragic history outlined in the stories of these Strongmen: the Holocaust and other mass murders committed by the Nazis; the Red Famine or Holodomor, Gulags, and Great Purge under Stalin; the massive repression, starvation, and tyranny of Mao Zedong's Great Leap Forward and Cultural Revolution; and Saddam Hussein's gassing of the Kurds and other crimes against humanity. These ghastly histories are not buried secrets waiting for some enterprising journalist or historian to uncover them. They are all too well documented. They took place in daylight, not darkness.

It would be comforting to believe Hitler's biographer Ian Kershaw when he wrote, "Mercifully, what happened in Germany in 1933, and its aftermath, will remain a uniquely terrible episode in history. . . . It also reminds us of the need for international cooperation to restrain potential 'mad dogs' in world politics before they are dangerous enough to bite."

Tragically, it is not correct to say that what Hitler and Nazi Germany did was "uniquely terrible." The histories of Stalin's Soviet Union and Mao's China after Hitler's defeat show that the Nazis were not the last of the "mad dogs." Other recent acts of mass murder, ethnic cleansing, and genocide since the Nazi era are different only in scale, not intent.

More significantly, the idea that acknowledging, studying, and remembering these past events will somehow prevent future catastrophes has not worked out so well. "Mad dogs" abound in the history of the world—before and since the events described in these five narratives.

It is worth retelling the story of a speech Adolf Hitler once delivered to his generals. The week before the invasion of Poland in 1939, which started the Second World War, Hitler met with his military leadership and offered what Samantha Power describes as a "notorious tutorial on a central lesson of the recent past: Victors write the history books." Hitler commented:

"It was knowingly and lightheartedly that Genghis Khan sent thousands of women to their deaths. History sees in him only the founder of a state. . . . The aim of war is not to reach definite lines but to annihilate the enemy physically. It is by this means that we shall obtain the vital living space that we need. *Who today still speaks of the massacre of the Armenians?*"

The Armenians spoken of by Hitler were the millions of people killed by Turkish general Enver Paşa, an ally of Germany during the First World War. Power also notes that Joseph Stalin made similar remarks while signing death warrants: "Who's going to remember all this riff-raff in ten or twenty years' time? No one."

Who today still speaks of the massacre of the Armenians?

The list of deadly dictatorships that have been responsible for millions of deaths is long. It certainly doesn't begin or end with the five examples outlined in this book. And sometimes it is not war or political ideology that creates such a murderous record.

In the late 1880s, as the European powers were scrambling to colonize and exploit the resources of Africa, King Leopold II of Belgium seized a vast and mostly unexplored territory surrounding the Congo River. Rich in rubber, the Congo became the scene of a grim, brutal pursuit of this increasingly vital resource. Under the rule of the Belgian kingdom, the Congolese people suffered rape, murder, starvation, and the amputation of limbs for failure to meet quotas of collecting rubber plants. The death toll from Leopold's brutal regime ultimately killed as many as ten million Congolese, all in the name of profits. It is a litany of destruction that makes the Congo "one of the major killing grounds of modern times," as historian Adam Hochschild wrote in *King Leopold's Ghost*, "a death toll of Holocaust dimensions."

And the list goes on. Hitler's allies, the Japanese led by Emperor Hirohito, who was not tried for war crimes, were ruthless in their subjugation of the Asian nations they made colonies during World War II. They raped, killed, and enslaved millions of people throughout Asia, notoriously forcing many women into sexual slavery as "comfort women" for Japanese soldiers. Tōjō Hideki, prime minister of Japan from 1941 to 1944, was deemed responsible for at least five million civilian deaths during the war. He was executed for war crimes in 1948.

The Communist leaders Ho Chi Minh of Vietnam and Pol Pot of Cambodia have also been blamed for millions of deaths.

In Africa, Idi Amin of Uganda was well known for his ruthlessness, but was often depicted somewhat comically during his eight years of rule from 1971 to 1979, and called Big Daddy.

While the numbers of his victims are debated, the Butcher of Uganda, as he was also known, used murder almost gleefully to eliminate enemies and assert a Strongman's control of his country. A former cook in the British Army, Amin targeted opponents—imagined or real—including other army officers, farmers, students, clerks, shopkeepers, government officials, and religious leaders such as the archbishop of the Church of Uganda. These victims were shot or forced to club one another to death, according to witnesses. As reported in his *New York Times* obituary, Idi Amin killed at least three hundred thousand Ugandans. Other accounts tell of enemies—including several of his own ministers—thrown to the crocodiles of Lake Victoria. He was never tried for these crimes and, after being deposed as dictator, escaped Uganda and finished his life comfortably in exile in Saudi Arabia before his death in 2003.

At the beginning of the twenty-first century, crimes against humanity continue to be committed. North Korea, Myanmar, China, and Syria stand accused of policies bordering on genocidal. In 2014, a former Syrian military photographer smuggled out thousands of photos and records documenting atrocities committed under the regime of President Bashar al-Assad. Stephen Rapp, the U.S. State Department's top war crimes official at the time, said it was "solid evidence of the kind of machinery of cruel death that we haven't seen frankly since the Nazis."

In a 2019 report on democracy around the world, the human

rights monitoring group Freedom House reported, "In Syria and Myanmar, hundreds of thousands of civilians from certain ethnic and religious groups have been killed or displaced as world powers either fail to respond adequately or facilitate the violence. Russia's occupation of Crimea has included targeted repression of Crimean Tatars and those who insist on maintaining their Ukrainian identity. China's mass internment of Uighurs and other Muslims—with some 800,000 to 2 million people held arbitrarily in 'reeducation' camps—can only be interpreted as a superpower's attempt to annihilate the distinct identities of minority groups."

Few places on earth equal the brutality of North Korea, where Kim Jong-Un is heir to a Communist dictatorship that has killed millions with the same mass starvation, labor camps, and executions typical of Hitler, Stalin, and Mao. Kim continues to build a nuclear arsenal and rules with extreme brutality, making his nation among the worst human rights violators in the world.

In North Korea, according to the United Nations, "these crimes against humanity entail extermination, murder, enslavement, torture, imprisonment, rape, forced abortions and other sexual violence, persecution on political, religious, racial and gender grounds, the forcible transfer of populations, the enforced disappearance of persons and the inhumane act of knowingly causing prolonged starvation." According to the report, which was prepared for the U.N. Human Rights Council and is more than three hundred pages long, North Korea "operates an all-encompassing indoctrination machine that takes root from childhood to propagate an official personality cult and to manufacture absolute obedience to the Supreme Leader."

North Korea's nuclear capability is worrisome, but its weapons, military forces, and economic powers are still dwarfed by Russia's under Vladimir Putin. In 2017, Putin became the longest-serving Russian leader since Joseph Stalin. A former officer in the KGB, or Soviet secret police, Putin was appointed prime minister in 1999 and was then elected to office in 2000. Since then, he has been able to change Russian laws permitting his reelection with almost no opposition. He has complete control over Russia's media outlets and has used propaganda, blackmail, prosecutions, and fear to virtually eliminate political opponents. In 2000, he began a ten-year military campaign that showed off his "take-no-prisoners" approach to power when he put down a rebellion by an Islamic separatist movement in the former Soviet republic of Chechnya. Deaths were estimated at twenty-five thousand to as many as a hundred thousand—a large number of them civilians.

Under his direction, Russia aggressively moved to take territory it claimed as its own in the Crimea and from Ukraine. Assassinations of journalists, and attempted assassinations of other dissidents, have all been linked back to Putin's Kremlin. And Putin has consolidated control of Russia's vast oil, chemical, and other natural resources for himself and loyal oligarchs. In doing so, he has become perhaps the world's richest man, with a net worth of $200 billion by one recent estimate, a figure that would make him wealthier than Amazon's Jeff Bezos and Microsoft's Bill Gates—put together.

And then there is the complicated role of Russia interfering with elections in Europe and in the United States. What was already clear to U.S. intelligence agencies in the months before the 2016 presidential election is that Russia was mounting a sustained attack on U.S. democracy. While the exact impact of the Russian hacking and secret influence is still being debated, journalists Scott Shane and Mark Mazzetti of the *New York Times* have concluded:

"The Russians carried out a landmark intervention that will be examined for decades to come. Acting on the personal animus of Mr. Putin, public and private instruments of Russian power moved with daring and skill to harness the currents of American politics. . . . The Russian intervention was essentially a hijacking—of American companies like Facebook and Twitter; of American citizens' feelings about immigration and race; of American journalists eager for scoops, however modest; of the naïve, or perhaps not so naïve, ambitions of Mr. Trump's advisers. The Russian trolls, hackers and agents totaled barely 100, and their task was to steer millions of American voters. They knew it would take a village to sabotage an election."

Vladimir Putin called the breakup of the Soviet Union a catastrophe, and many feel he is trying to re-create the former Stalinist empire. This is what Russian-born journalist Masha Gessen means in the title of her book *The Future Is History: How Totalitarianism Reclaimed Russia*. It is sobering to read that despite the revelations of Stalin's murderous legacy, the former dictator is greatly admired. In a 2003 poll asking Russians to name the "greatest people who have ever lived,"

40 percent of the respondents said Stalin, and 21 percent said Putin. Asked the same question five years later, 32 percent of the respondents put Putin among the greatest-ever people, while 36 percent named Stalin.

It might be useful to think about authoritarianism, totalitarianism, or any kind of dictatorship in the same way we think about dangerous, life-threatening, infectious diseases. The best prevention against such a disease is to build immunity. Education is like a vaccination. Understanding history is part of the process of making ourselves more immune to the dangers of dictatorship.

Learning from the experience of history requires recognizing the patterns of dictatorships—the Strongman's Playbook. Each of these profiles has laid out a set of steps that go into the making of a dictatorship. This blueprint typically includes the following:

- ★ **Extreme nationalism that calls for restoring a country's past glory or greatness.**
- ★ **Placing blame on a single group—usually an ethnic or religious minority, or foreign threat.**
- ★ **Warning of an emergency, often nonexistent, or responding to severe economic distress that threatens the nation.**
- ★ **Calls for "law and order" and eliminating corruption.**

Once in a position of power, the Strongman does some or all of the following:

- ☆ Moves to control the courts, legislature, and elections.

- ☆ Heightens an emergency that may not exist.

- ☆ Creates a crisis that may demand military intervention.

- ☆ Takes control of the media.

- ☆ Increases the use of propaganda.

- ☆ Jails or threatens opponents, including journalists.

- ☆ Attacks artists, intellectuals, and other free thinkers.

- ☆ Sets out to control the education system.

- ☆ Attempts to create a young generation of devoted followers.

- ☆ Doles out economic favors to supporters and allies.

- ☆ Creates a larger-than-life cult of personality.

- ☆ Either threatens or restricts religious freedom, or bends religion to the regime's agenda.

Most of the leaders discussed in this history practiced and perfected all of these techniques, taking them to inhumane depths. But the Strongman does not have to kill millions to accomplish his goals. Authoritarian governments do not always need concentration camps, mass starvation, or genocidal wars to maintain their power. In an age in which information has become the prevailing weapon of choice, the person who controls the flow of opinions, news, and facts may hold the greatest power.

The United States of America, unlike the countries discussed in this book that have seen the rise of a Strongman, has a much older democratic and republican tradition. Its roots lie in a Constitution and body of laws, courts, and free press that serve as the guardrails to keep the country free of an authoritarian despot. While the country's progress in giving democratic power to all citizens has often been painfully slow and frequently unjust, it has certainly evolved from what the framers envisioned in 1787. Every step along the way to greater freedom and justice has required people who were willing to go against the grain, in ending slavery, winning the vote for women, and expanding civil rights. These battles are far from over. While the United States has not yet succumbed to a Strongman, the price of democracy is vigilance, even in the face of crisis or daunting odds.

Is it worth it?

Confronting the uncertainty and despairing mood in the midst of the Second World War, a federal agency called the Writers' War Board asked the *New Yorker* magazine to answer the question "What is democracy?" Here's the answer of essayist E. B. White, the future author of *Charlotte's Web*:

"Surely the Board knows what democracy is. It is the line that forms on the right. It is the don't in don't shove. . . . Democracy is the recurrent suspicion that more than half of the people are right more than half of the time. It is the feeling of privacy in the voting booths, the feeling of communion in the libraries, the feeling of vitality everywhere. Democracy is a letter to the editor. Democracy is the score at the beginning of the ninth. It is an idea which hasn't been disproved yet, a song the words of which have not gone bad. It's the mustard on the hot dog and the cream in the rationed coffee. Democracy is a request from a War Board, in the middle of a morning in the middle of a war, wanting to know what democracy is."

And he was right. There is sanctity in the voting booth. Involved citizens not only vote in elections, but also can—and should—take part in other aspects of civic engagement: to call, write, or email elected officials is a right; to voice an opinion in the newspapers with a letter to the editor is a right; to march nonviolently, to protest, to strike, and to boycott are all rights to be cherished, protect, preserved, but most of all exercised.

These are the invaluable liberties and powerful tools that have helped advance the cause of such issues as abolition, suffrage, civil rights, marriage equality, and other issues on which many people still disagree, such as gun laws and reproductive rights. And there is no age requirement for joining a protest or speaking your mind. Across the world, teenagers are leading the climate change movement, and in the United States young students—some of them victims of mass school shootings—have mobilized a movement for safer gun laws. Not by accident, that movement is called Never Again.

Americans are fortunate to still enjoy the freedom of expression and protest. But as the five stories in this book prove, the guardrails built to protect those rights are removable. A free press can be silenced. Courts can be tilted in favor of one ideology. The powerful can buy access that the average person cannot afford. Freedom to protest can be restrained. Laws can be revised or rewritten to take away rights. Once they are gone, such rights are difficult to resuscitate.

In answering questions about the rise of the Strongman, we are left with some other hard questions. Do you pay attention to the laws being made locally and nationally? Do you expect and demand that your representatives pay attention to you? Do you pay attention to what judges and courts are saying? Do you support a vigorous, independent free press that holds officials accountable? Can you recognize the difference between fact and opinion? Do you work to support, protect, and expand voting rights—the rights that many people have struggled, bled, and even died for?

Do you think for yourself? Do you question authority?

Resistance to powerful forces of authoritarianism is difficult and dangerous, as so many of these stories have shown. The simple truth is that many people, if not most people, are willing to do what they are told and are willing to do what the crowd does. They do not question or challenge authority. It is a basic aspect of human psychology. People often "go along to get along." But one of historian Timothy Snyder's takeaways from the story of twentieth-century tyranny is "Do not obey in advance."

In Germany, the World War I veteran and Lutheran minister Martin Niemöller initially welcomed Hitler's accession to power. Niemöller gradually abandoned those views and became aware that the Gestapo was watching him. Between 1934 and 1937, he was arrested and released seven times. Finally, the Gestapo picked him up, convicted him of making "treasonable statements," and sent him to the concentration camps. He spent seven years in the camps before he was liberated by U.S. troops. He is best known today for this quotation:

"First they came for the socialists, and I did not speak out— because I was not a socialist. Then they came for the trade unionists, and I did not speak out—because I was not a trade unionist. Then they came for the Jews, and I did not speak out— because I was not a Jew. Then they came for me—and there was no one left to speak for me."

According to the U.S. Holocaust Memorial Museum, the quotation is derived from Niemöller's lectures following the war: "Much controversy surrounds the content of the poem as it has been printed in varying forms, referring to diverse groups such as Catholics, Jehovah's Witnesses, Jews, Trade Unionists, or Communists depending upon the version. Nonetheless his point was that Germans had been complicit through their silence in the Nazi imprisonment, persecution, and murder of millions of people. He felt this was true in particular of the leaders of the Protestant churches (of which the Lutheran church was one denomination)."

Niemöller may have come to his realization slowly, but he spent much of his later life trying to make amends for his own anti-Semitism and support of the Nazis. Despite his early failings, he was still a rare person who saw what was happening in Germany. Even more rare were the heroic figures who spoke out and took action when they began to witness the growing tyranny, such as Hans and Sophie Scholl and the other White Rose members. "I acted as I had to act," said Kurt Huber, another young German executed for his White Rose activities, "prompted by a voice that came from within."

In the famous novel *Lord of the Flies*, a group of British schoolboys is left marooned on an island after a plane crash. Their attempts at order and the rule of law—symbolized by the conch shell that allows whoever holds it to speak—soon descend into murderous, tribal savagery in a struggle for power. Initially chosen "chief," a boy named Ralph tries to maintain order but becomes a solitary voice, ultimately forced to fight for his life as the others fall to the appeal of a Strongman.

History sadly shows that there are few Ralphs and few Hans and Sophie Scholls.

In the beloved children's book *The Cat in the Hat*, after two children spend an afternoon of chaos and messiness with a mischievous cat while their mother is out, a boy wonders whether he and his sister, Sally, should tell her what took place. His question is the same one that these terrible stories force us to ask:

"What would YOU do if your mother asked YOU?"

ACKNOWLEDGMENTS

For more than thirty years, I have been writing books about history. During that time, I have often had to describe how dreadful the past can be. To explain American slavery and its devastating consequences, or to trace the long, tragic chronicle of the destruction of Native American nations, is to come face-to-face with a harsh truth: history overflows with cruelty and evil. Sadly, we must boldly and honestly tell these stories of the violence that people can inflict on other people. Of course, that side of the ledger should also be weighed against the slow progress that has been made over the centuries toward a more just and equitable world.

Yet, in many ways, this book has been the most difficult one for me to research and write. The sheer weight of these horrific stories is a heavy burden. For much of my adult life, I maintained a somewhat optimistic outlook. I kept faith in the belief, voiced by Martin Luther King Jr. and borrowed from the earlier words of abolitionist Theodore Parker: "The arc of the moral universe is long, but it bends toward justice."

Unfortunately, the accounts of inhumanity that accompany the life stories and times of these Strongmen profoundly test that belief. Having completed this book, I confess that my own hopes for a fairer, more peaceful future have been darkened by the unforgiving reality described in this book. As democracy has been in retreat around the world during the early years of the twenty-first century, a gloomy pessimism has fallen over the world. The famous measure of whether we see a glass half-full or half-empty has edged ominously toward the empty side.

But as 2019 came to a close, some flickers of democracy's light began to shine in the darkness. People have taken to the streets to give new voice to democratic dreams. As I write this, the outcome of their struggles is far from settled and the future of democracy is still under severe stress. So I will say I am not thoroughly pessimistic, but alarmed. The alarm bells are ringing and it is a question of how we as individuals respond to the alarms.

I am extremely grateful to Macmillan and Holt Books for allowing me to sound this alarm. This is an opportunity to make this hard history a bit more understandable, especially to young people. And I would especially like to thank my editor, Brian Geffen, who supported this project with great enthusiasm. Also many thanks to the Holt Books/Macmillan team, including Christian Trimmer, Jean Feiwel, Molly Ellis, Alexei Esikoff, Katie Halata, Kristen Luby, Patrick Collins, Aurora Parlagreco, Jie Yang, Angela Jun, Kay Petronio, and Rachel Murray. I would like to especially thank Sherri Schmidt and Jennifer Healey for their rigorous and valuable work of editing.

I am also indebted to many great institutions, starting with the New York Public Library, the Library of Congress, and the United States Holocaust Museum and Memorial for their work in keeping these stories alive and accessible to all. Other institutions I have visited, such as the *Fondazione Ex-Campo Fossoli* (Camp Fossoli Foundation) and the Museum of the Deported in Carpi, Italy, also help focus attention on this hard history and how some people have responded heroically to repression and genocide. Many such museums, memorials, and historic sites can be found through the organization "Sites of Conscience."

During the past few years, I have also come to know and work with a great many social studies educators, including Tina Haefner, Larry Paska, and other officers and members of the National Council for the Social Studies (NCSS), which has elevated the question of civics education to a high priority. There is much work to be done, but I would like to thank them for their hard work, dedication, and devotion to their students and the fundamental significance of civic engagement.

I have also come to know many educators over the past few years as I have visited schools and spoke at teacher conferences, and I am grateful to Jessica Ellison and many other people working to bring history to young people.

As always, I am ever grateful for the support of my family. Thanks to Colin Davis for his insights, Jenny Davis for her considerable expertise and suggestions, and my wife, Joann Davis, always my greatest supporter and most exacting reader.

BIBLIOGRAPHY

Many of the sources listed here are works of history written for the adult audience, which are generally excellent reference works for young adult readers. Asterisks (*) denote books that are aimed specifically at young adults or that I consider particularly appropriate for readers in middle school and high school.

GENERAL READINGS AND RESOURCES

Albright, Madeleine. *Fascism: A Warning*. New York: HarperCollins, 2018.

Amar, Akhil Reed. *America's Constitution: A Biography*. New York: Random House, 2006.

——. *The Bill of Rights: Creation and Reconstruction*. New Haven, CT: Yale University Press, 1998.

Arendt, Hannah. *The Origins of Totalitarianism*. New York: Harvest Books, 1994.

*Bailey, Diane. *Democracy*. Major Forms of World Government. Broomall, PA: Mason Crest, 2013.

Beard, Mary. *SPQR: A History of Ancient Rome*. New York: Liveright, 2015.

Boorstin, Daniel. *The Discoverers: A History of Man's Search to Know His World and Himself*. New York: Random House, 1983.

Brendon, Piers. *The Dark Valley: A Panorama of the 1930s*. New York: Knopf, 2000.

Cartledge, Paul. *Democracy: A Life*. New York: Oxford University Press, 2016.

Chang, Gordon G. *The Coming Collapse of China*. New York: Random House, 2001.

*Davis, Kenneth C. *America's Hidden History: Untold Tales of the First Pilgrims, Fighting Women, and Forgotten Founders Who Shaped a Nation*. New York: Smithsonian Books, 2008.

*——. *Don't Know Much About History: Everything You Need to Know About American History but Never Learned*. New York: Harper, 2012.

*——. *The Hidden History of America at War: Untold Tales from Yorktown to Fallujah*. New York: Hachette, 2015.

Dunn, John. *Democracy: A History*. New York: Atlantic Monthly Press, 2005.

Eatwell, Roger. *Fascism: A History*. London: Pimlico, 2003.

Ferguson, Niall. *Civilization: The West and the Rest*. New York: Penguin Books, 2011.

*Freedman, Russell. *The War to End All Wars: World War I*. Boston: Clarion Books, 2010.

Gessen, Masha. *The Man Without a Face: The Unlikely Rise of Vladimir Putin*. New York: Riverhead Books, 2012.

——. *The Future Is History: How Totalitarianism Reclaimed Russia*. New York: Riverhead Books, 2017.

*Gombrich, E. H. *A Little History of the World*. Illus. ed. Translated by Caroline Mustill. New Haven, CT: Yale University Press, 2011.

*Greenberg, Ellen. *The House and the Senate Explained: The People's Guide to Congress*. New York: Norton, 1996.

*——. *The Supreme Court Explained*. New York: Norton, 1997.

Hamilton, Alexander. *Writings*. New York: Library of America, 2001.

Harari, Yuval Noah. *Sapiens: A Brief History of Mankind*. New York: Harper, 2015.

Hastings, Max. *Inferno: The World at War, 1939–1945*. New York: Vintage, 2012.

Hochschild, Adam. *King Leopold's Ghost: A Story of Greed, Terror, and Heroism in Africa*. Boston: Houghton Mifflin, 1998.

Hughes, Robert. *Rome: A Cultural, Visual, and Personal History*. New York: Vintage, 2012.

Isikoff, Michael, and David Corn. *Russian Roulette: The Inside Story of Putin's War on America and the Election of Donald Trump*. New York: Twelve/Hachette, 2018.

*Jünger, Ernst. *Storm of Steel*. Translated by Michael Hofmann. New York: Penguin Books, 2016.

Lemkin, Raphael. *Axis Rule in Occupied Europe*. Washington, D.C.: Carnegie Endowment for International Peace, 1944. https://babel.hathitrust.org/cgi /pt?id=mdp.39015005077436&view=1up&seq=11

*Levinson, Cynthia, and Sanford Levinson. *Fault Lines in the Constitution: The Framers, Their Fights, and the Flaws That Affect Us Today*. Atlanta: Peachtree, 2019.

Levitsky, Steven, and Daniel Ziblatt. *How Democracies Die*. New York: Crown, 2018.

Machiavelli, Niccolò. *The Prince*. Translated by George Bull. New York: Penguin, 1999.

Mounk, Yascha. *The People vs. Democracy: Why Our Freedom Is in Danger and How to Save It*. Cambridge, MA: Harvard University Press, 2018.

Orwell, George. *1984*. New York: Harcourt, 1949.

Plato. *Republic*. Translated by Robin Waterfield. New York: Oxford University Press, 1993.

Power, Samantha. *"A Problem from Hell": America and the Age of Genocide*. New York: Basic Books, 2013.

Smith, Adam. *An Inquiry into the Nature and Causes of the Wealth of Nations*. London, 1776.

*Snyder, Timothy. *On Tyranny: Twenty Lessons from the Twentieth Century*. New York: Tim Duggan Books, 2017.

———. *The Road to Unfreedom: Russia, Europe, America*. New York: Tim Duggan Books, 2018.

Stanley, Jason. *How Propaganda Works*. Princeton, NJ: Princeton University Press, 2015.

———. *How Fascism Works: The Politics of Us and Them*. New York: Random House, 2018.

Sunstein, Cass, ed. *Can It Happen Here? Authoritarianism in America.* New York: Dey Street/William Morrow, 2018.

Tocqueville, Alexis de. *Democracy in America.* Edited by J. P. Mayer. Translated by George Lawrence. New York: Harper Perennial, 1969.

Todd, Allan. *The European Dictatorships: Hitler, Stalin, Mussolini.* New York: Cambridge University Press, 2002.

*Tribe, Laurence H., and Michael C. Dorf. *On Reading the Constitution.* Cambridge, MA: Harvard University Press, 1991.

Watts, Edward J. *Mortal Republic: How Rome Fell into Tyranny.* New York: Basic Books, 2018.

Wood, Gordon S. *The Radicalism of the American Revolution.* New York: Vintage Books, 1993.

MUSSOLINI

Bosworth, R. J. B. *Mussolini: New Edition.* New York: Bloomsbury, 2010.

———. *Mussolini's Italy: Life Under Fascist Dictatorship 1915–1945.* New York: Penguin Books, 2006.

*Hartenian, Larry. *Benito Mussolini.* New York: Chelsea House, 1988.

Hibbert, Christopher. *Il Duce: The Life of Benito Mussolini.* Boston: Little, Brown, 1962.

Kertzer, David I. *The Pope and Mussolini: The Secret History of Pius XI and the Rise of Fascism in Europe.* New York: Random House, 2014.

*Levi, Primo. *Survival in Auschwitz: The Nazi Assault on Humanity.* Translated by Stuart Woolf. New York: Touchstone, 1996.

Luzzatto, Sergio. *The Body of Il Duce: Mussolini's Corpse and the Fortunes of Italy.* Translated by Frederika Randall. New York: Metropolitan Books, 2005.

Ridley, Jasper. *Mussolini: A Biography.* New York: St. Martin's, 1997.

HITLER

*Bartoletti, Susan Campbell. *Hitler Youth: Growing Up in Hitler's Shadow.* New York: Scholastic, 2005.

Dumbach, Annette, and Jud Newborn. *Sophie Scholl and the White Rose*. 75th anniversary edition. Oxford, UK: Oneworld, 2018.

Evans, Richard J. *The Coming of the Third Reich*. New York: Penguin, 2004.

———. *The Third Reich in Power*. New York: Penguin, 2006.

———. *The Third Reich at War*. New York: Penguin, 2009.

Fest, Joachim C. *Hitler*. Translated by Richard and Clara Winston. New York: Harcourt Brace, 1974.

*Freedman, Russell. *We Will Not Be Silent: The White Rose Student Resistance Movement That Defied Adolf Hitler*. New York: Clarion Books, 2016.

Ham, Paul. *Young Hitler: The Making of the Führer*. New York: Pegasus Books, 2018.

Hamann, Brigitte. *Hitler's Vienna: A Dictator's Apprenticeship*. Translated by Thomas Thornton. New York: Oxford University Press, 1999.

Hett, Benjamin Carter. *The Death of Democracy: Hitler's Rise to Power and the Downfall of the Weimar Republic*. New York: Henry Holt, 2018.

Hitler, Adolf. *Mein Kampf*. Trans. Ralph Manheim. Boston: Houghton Mifflin, 1943.

Kater, Michael H. *Hitler Youth*. Cambridge, MA: Harvard University Press, 2004.

Kershaw, Ian. *Hitler: A Biography*. New York: Norton, 2008. Abridgement of *Hitler, 1889–1936* (published in 1999) and *Hitler, 1936–1945* (published in 2000).

Lyman, Robert. *Under a Darkening Sky: The American Experience in Nazi Europe: 1939–1941*. New York: Pegasus Books, 2018.

Scholl, Inge. *The White Rose: Munich 1942–1943*. Translated by Arthur R. Schultz. Middletown, CT: Wesleyan University Press, 1983.

Snyder, Timothy. *Bloodlands: Europe Between Hitler and Stalin*. New York: Basic Books, 2010.

Weber, Thomas. *Becoming Hitler: The Making of a Nazi*. New York: Basic Books, 2017.

Whitman, James Q. *Hitler's American Model: The United States and the Making of Nazi Race Law*. Princeton, NJ: Princeton University Press, 2017.

STALIN

Applebaum, Anne. *Red Famine: Stalin's War on Ukraine*. New York: Penguin, 2017.

Conquest, Robert. *The Great Terror: A Reassessment*. New York: Oxford University Press, 1990.

Khlevniuk, Oleg V. *Stalin: New Biography of a Dictator*. Translated by Nora Seligman Favorov. New Haven, CT: Yale University Press, 2015.

Kotkin, Stephen. *Stalin: Waiting for Hitler, 1929–1941*. New York: Penguin, 2017.

Montefiore, Simon Sebag. *Young Stalin*. New York: Knopf, 2007.

Remnick, David. *Lenin's Tomb: The Last Days of the Soviet Empire*. New York: Vintage Books, 1994.

Service, Robert. *Stalin: A Biography*. Cambridge, MA: Harvard University Press, 2005.

Solzhenitsyn, Aleksandr. *The Gulag Archipelago 1918—1956: An Experiment in Literary Investigation*. Vol. 1. Translated by Thomas P. Whitney. New York: Harper & Row, 1974.

*———. *One Day in the Life of Ivan Denisovich*. Translated by H. T. Willetts. New York: Farrar, Straus and Giroux, 1991.

*Yelchin, Eugene. *Breaking Stalin's Nose*. New York: Henry Holt, 2011.

MAO ZEDONG

*Chen, Da. *China's Son: Growing Up in the Cultural Revolution*. New York: Delacorte, 2001.

Dikötter, Frank. *The Cultural Revolution: A People's History, 1962–1976*. New York: Bloomsbury, 2016.

Griffin, Nicholas. *Ping-Pong Diplomacy: The Secret History Behind the Game That Changed the World*. New York: Scribner, 2014.

*Heuston, Kimberley. *Mao Zedong*. New York: Scholastic, 2010.

*Jiang, Ji-li. *Red Scarf Girl: A Memoir of the Cultural Revolution*. New York: HarperCollins, 1997.

*Li, Moying. *Snow Falling in Spring: Coming of Age in China During the Cultural Revolution*. New York: Farrar, Straus and Giroux, 2008.

Roberts, J. A. G. *A Short History of China*. 2nd ed. New York: Palgrave Macmillan, 2006.

Short, Philip. *Mao: The Man Who Made China*. Rev. ed. London: I. B. Taurus, 2017.

Terrill, Ross. *Mao: A Biography*. Revised and expanded edition. Redwood City, CA: Stanford University Press, 1999.

SADDAM HUSSEIN

Munthe, Turi, ed. *The Saddam Hussein Reader: Selections from Leading Writers on Iraq*. New York: Thunder's Mouth Press, 2002.

Makiya, Kanan. *Republic of Fear: The Politics of Modern Iraq*. Berkeley: University of California Press, 1998.

Myerson, Daniel. *Blood and Splendor: The Lives of Five Tyrants, from Nero to Saddam Hussein*. New York: HarperCollins, 2000.

Newton, Michael A., and Michael P. Scharf. *Enemy of the State: The Trial and Execution of Saddam Hussein*. New York: St. Martin's Press, 2008.

Salbi, Zainab, and Laurie Becklund. *Between Two Worlds: Escape from Tyranny; Growing Up in the Shadow of Saddam*. New York: Gotham Books, 2005.

NOTES

Introduction: Dictators, Despots, and Democracy

1   The leader of a tyrannical regime: "Saddam Hussein, Hitler, Stalin, Mao, & More: 13 Deadliest Dictators (Photos)," *Daily Beast*, July 13, 2017, thedailybeast.com/saddam -hussein-hitler-stalin-mao-and-more-13-deadliest-dictators-photos.

2   In March 2020: Freedom House, *Freedom in the World 2020: A Leaderless Struggle for Democracy*, https://freedomhouse.org/report/freedom-world/2020/leaderless-struggle -democracy.

Chapter 1: Democracy in Flames

3   On a cold night in Germany's capital: The Reichstag fire and Hitler's reaction to it are recounted in Hett, *The Death of Democracy*, pp. 1–2.

4   near-hysteria: Kershaw, *Hitler*, p. 277.

5   "defiant protest": Kershaw, *Hitler*, p. 274.

6   With guarantees of religious freedom: Hett, *The Death of Democracy*, p. 7.

7   "One had to buy quickly": George Grosz, *A Little Yes and a Big NO*, trans. L. S. Dorin (New York: Dial, 1946), p. 124, in Facing History and Ourselves, "Personal Accounts of the Inflation Years (1919–1924)," Weimar Republic: The Fragility of Democracy, facinghistory.org/weimar-republic-fragility-democracy/economics/personal-accounts -inflation-years-economics-1919-1924-inflation.

8   "By some estimates": Kershaw, *Hitler*, p. 196.

9   "political earthquake": Kershaw, *Hitler*, p. 204.

10 Nazi storm troopers went on a tear: Hett, *The Death of Democracy*, p. 3.

11 "The violence and repression": Kershaw, pp. 276–277.

12 "First the Reichstag burned": Walther Kiaulehn, *Berlin: Schicksaleiner Weltstadt* (Munich: C. H. Beck, 1997), p. 344, in Hett, *The Death of Democracy* p. 6.

Chapter 2: "Let Arms Yield to the Toga"

13 "If men were angels": *Federalist* No. 51, Feb. 6, 1788, Founders Online, National Archives, founders.archives.gov/documents/Hamilton/01-04-02-0199.

14 "The people are turbulent and changing": Alexander Hamilton, speech in convention, cited in Hamilton, *Writings*, p. 164.

15 "The evils we experience": U.S. Constitutional Convention, *The Debates in the Federal Convention of 1787 Which Framed the Constitution of the United States of America*, reported by James Madison, eds. James Brown Scott and Gaillard Hunt (New York: Oxford University Press, 1920), p. 32, hdl.handle.net/2027/mdp.35112104842812.

16 "In a state which is desirous of being saved": Plato, *Laws*, in *The Dialogues of Plato* vol. 4, trans. B. Jowett (New York, 1897), p. 269.

17 *Tyrant* comes from the Greek *tyrannos*: Online Etymology Dictionary, s.v. "tyrant," etymonline.com/word/tyrant.

18 "Attempting to fix the system": Russell Meiggs, "Cleisthenes of Athens," *Encyclopaedia Britannica*, britannica.com/biography/Cleisthenes-of-Athens.

19 Meeting at least once a month: Mark Cartwright, "Athenian Democracy," Ancient History Encyclopedia, April 3, 2018, ancient.eu/Athenian_Democracy/.

20 "Our form of government does not": *Thucydides*, trans. Benjamin Jowett (Oxford, 1881), 2.37, data.perseus.org/citations/urn:cts:greekLit:tlg0003.tlg001.perseus-eng2:2.37.

21 When King Philip II of neighboring Macedonia: Christopher W. Blackwell, "Athenian Democracy: A Brief Overview," *Dēmos*, February 28, 2003, stoa.org/demos/article _democracy_overview@page=all&greekEncoding=UnicodeC.html.

22 The word *republic* comes from the Latin *respublica*: Online Etymology Dictionary, s.v. "republic," etymonline.com/word/republic.

23 "born slowly over a period of decades": Beard, *SPQR*, p. 131.

24 "In the early years of the Republic": Hughes, *Rome*, p. 31.

25 "The city on the Tiber": Hughes, *Rome*, p. 25.

26 Samuel Adams used Cedant Arma Togae: Noel Bertram Gerson, *The Grand Incendiary: A Biography of Samuel Adams* (New York: Dial Press, 1973), p. 100, in Carl J. Richard, "Cicero and the American Founders," in *Brill's Companion to the Reception of Cicero*, ed. William H. F. Altman (Leiden, NL: Brill, 2015), p. 129.

27 In Boston on March 5, 1775: Warren's role in the early days of the Revolution is told more thoroughly in the chapter "Warren's Toga" in my 2008 book, *America's Hidden History*.

28 "The founders considered the Roman Republic": Hope Grossman, "Classicism," Digital Encyclopedia of George Washington, Center for Digital History at the Washington Library, Mount Vernon, mountvernon.org/library/digitalhistory/digital-encyclopedia/article/classicism/.

29 "All this was breathtakingly novel": Amar, *America's Constitution*, p. 8.

30 "The world must be made safe for democracy": President Wilson's Declaration of War Message to Congress, April 2, 1917, Records of the U.S. Senate, Record Group 46, National Archives, ourdocuments.gov/doc.php?flash=false&doc=61&page=transcript.

Chapter 3: "Believe, Obey, and Fight"

31 "The overall array of weaponry": Blaine Taylor, "How Mussolini Took Power (and Destroyed Italy)," reprinted from Warfare History Network by *Buzz* (blog), Feb. 4, 2018, National Interest, nationalinterest.org/blog/the-buzz/how-mussolini-took-power -destroyed-italy-24330.

32 Fascist creed: Bosworth, *Mussolini's Italy*, p. 11.

33 "Our program is simple": Bosworth, *Mussolini*, p. 138.

34 That same morning Italy's king: *Encyclopaedia Britannica*, s.v. "March on Rome," updated Oct. 21, 2018, britannica.com/event/March-on-Rome.

35 "The truth was more mundane": Levitsky and Ziblatt, *How Democracies Die*, pp. 12–13.

36 "They saw Mussolini": Albright, *Fascism*, p. 23.

37 "Every man, as long as he does not violate the laws of justice": Smith, *Wealth of Nations*, bk. 4, ch. 9.

38 "The history of all hitherto existing society": Karl Marx and Frederick Engels, *Manifesto of the Communist Party*, trans. Samuel Moore, ed. Frederick Engels (Chicago, 1888), pt. 1, oll.libertyfund.org/pages/marx-manifesto.

39 he once stabbed a schoolmate: Bosworth, *Mussolini*, pp. 46–47.

40 "I want to teach men": Friedrich Nietzsche, *Thus Spake Zarathustra*, trans. Thomas

Common, vol. 11, *The Complete Works of Friedrich Nietzsche*, ed. Oscar Levy (New York: Macmillan, 1909), prologue pt. 7, p. 16.

41   "From today onward": Benito Mussolini, *Il Popolo d'Italia*, May 23, 1915, in John Foot and Christopher Hibbert, "Benito Mussolini," *Encyclopaedia Britannica*, updated July 25, 2019, britannica.com/biography/Benito-Mussolini.

42   Mussolini was hospitalized for months: Bosworth, *Mussolini,* p. 97.

43   "honorary loser": Bosworth, *Mussolini,* p. 107.

44   "ruthless and energetic enough": Hibbert, *Il Duce,* p. 24.

45   "only the intelligent and the strong-willed": Bosworth, *Mussolini,* p. 120.

46   "Populists are antiestablishment politicians": This quote and following warning signs of an authoritarian are from Levitsky and Ziblatt, *How Democracies Die*, pp. 21–24.

47   "banned rival parties": Bosworth, *Mussolini's Italy,* pp. 1–2.

48   Despite evidence that Matteotti had been killed: Alexander Stille recounts the Matteotti killing and its aftermath in "What a Murder by Mussolini Teaches Us About Khashoggi and M.B.S.," *New York Times*, Oct. 23, 2018, nyti.ms/2AoLnzO.

49   "all is for the state": Benito Mussolini, *Opera Omnia*, vol. 21, p. 425, in Bosworth, *Mussolini's Italy,* p. 215.

50   The Fascist-controlled government: Kertzer, *The Pope and Mussolini*, p. 144.

51   "Fascism is not a party but a religion": Bosworth, *Mussolini's Italy,* p. 233.

52   "fidelity to the King": Stefano Giani, "The Italian University Professors' Oath of Allegiance to Fascism (1931)," *Blog Nostrum*, April 11, 2017, blognostrumuva .wordpress.com/2017/04/11/the-italian-university-professors-oath-of-allegiance-to -fascism-1931/.

53   After the fighting in World War I ended: Marc Raboy, "15 Surprising Facts About Guglielmo Marconi, the Man Behind Radio Communication," *OUPblog*, Aug. 24, 2016, Oxford University Press, blog.oup.com/2016/08/15-facts-guglielmo-marconi/.

54   "to further the genius of our race": Rory Carroll, "Marconi Blocked Jews from Il Duce's Academy," *Guardian* (Manchester, UK), March 19, 2002, theguardian.com/world/2002 /mar/19/physicalsciences.humanities.

55   "The intent was twofold": Simon Martin, "World Cup Stunning Moments: Mussolini's Blackshirts' 1938 Win," *Guardian* (Manchester, UK), April 5, 2018, theguardian.com /football/blog/2014/apr/01/world-cup-moments-1938-italy-benito-mussolini.

56   The last of their Ten Commandments: Hughes, *Rome*, p. 413.

57   "The contest was hopelessly unequal": Hughes, *Rome*, p. 433.

58   "All took leave from life": Levi, *Survival in Auschwitz*, p. 15.

59   "Power tends to corrupt": Lord Acton to Archbishop Creighton, April 5, 1887, *Acton -Creighton Correspondence (1887)*, Online Library of Liberty, oll.libertyfund.org/ titles/2254.

Chapter 4: The Big Lie

60   an "Aryan" master race: *Encyclopaedia Britannica*, s.v. "Aryan," updated March 14, 2019, britannica.com/topic/Aryan.

61   "When Owens finished competing": Larry Schwartz, "Owens Pierced a Myth," ESPN SportsCentury, Dec. 30, 1999, espn.com/sportscentury/features/00016393.html.

62   "Hitler's Germany was open to viewing": Kershaw, *Hitler*, p. 359.

63   "biggest and showiest athletic contest ever staged": "National Physical Training Urged by Brundage for U.S. Athletes," *New York Times*, Aug. 19, 1936, nyti.ms/34JM97M.

64   having hundreds of his political rivals assassinated: U.S. Holocaust Memorial Museum, "Röhm Purge," Holocaust Encyclopedia, encyclopedia.ushmm.org/content/en/article/roehm-purge.

65   "The personality cult built around Hitler": Kershaw, *Hitler*, p. 262.

66   "It is impossible to imagine": Ham, *Young Hitler*, p. 11.

67   "pompous, status-proud, strict": Kershaw, *Hitler*, p. 3.

68   "If he didn't have his way he got very angry": Quoted in Norbert Bromberg and Verna Volz Small, *Hitler's Psychopathology* (New York: International Universities Press, 1983), p. 41, in Ham, *Young Hitler*, p. 15.

69   Hitler had used it as toilet paper: Ham, *Young Hitler*, p. 18.

70   "parasitic idleness": Kershaw, *Hitler*, p. 10.

71   "At thirteen, fourteen, fifteen": Adolf Hitler, Feb. 20–21, 1942, *Monologe in Führerhauptquartier, 1941–1944,* ed. Werner Jochmann (Hamburg, 1980), in Hamann, *Hitler's Vienna*, p. 19.

72   While in Vienna, Hitler was introduced: U.S. Holocaust Memorial Museum, "Adolf Hitler: Early Years, 1889–1913," Holocaust Encyclopedia, encyclopedia.ushmm.org/content/en/article/adolf-hitler-early-years-1889-1913.

73   "Greater Vienna must not turn into Greater Jerusalem!": Quoted in Hamann, *Hitler's Vienna*, p. 281.

74   "fighting to defend Christianity": Ham, *Young Hitler*, p. 61.

75   "unsuitable for military service": Ham, *Young Hitler*, p. 69.

76   "You will be home": Quoted in Hochschild, *King Leopold's Ghost*, p. 102.

77   "We had bonded together": Jünger, *Storm of Steel*, p. 5.

78   Once a shell struck: Kershaw, *Hitler*, pp. 54–57.

79   He was lying in a military hospital: Kershaw, *Hitler*, p. 60.

80   "greatest villainy of the century": Hitler, *Mein Kampf*, p. 202.

81   "The First World War made Hitler possible": Kershaw, *Hitler*, p. 47.

82   "He immediately found he could strike a chord": Kershaw, *Hitler*, p. 74.

83   He was spoken of as Germany's Mussolini: Kershaw, *Hitler*, p. 78.

84   "Here was a messiah-like figure": Ham, *Young Hitler*, p. 175.

85   *"Protocols* 'describes' the 'secret plans' of Jews": U.S. Holocaust Memorial Museum, "Protocols of the Elders of Zion," Holocaust Encyclopedia, encyclopedia.ushmm.org/content/en/article/protocols-of-the-elders-of-zion.

86   "significant religious symbol of our remote ancestors": U.S. Holocaust Memorial Museum, "The History of the Swastika," Aug. 17, 2017, Holocaust Encyclopedia, encyclopedia.ushmm.org/content/en/article/history-of-the-swastika.

87   "A curiously nasty, obscene odor": Fest, *Hitler,* p. 204.

88   The putsch failure convinced: U.S. Holocaust Memorial Museum, "Beer Hall Putsch (Munich Putsch)," Holocaust Encyclopedia, encyclopedia.ushmm.org/content/en/article/beer-hall-putsch-munich-putsch.

89   "What Hitler did was advertise unoriginal ideas": Kershaw, *Hitler*, p. 80.

90   Germany's economic crisis continued: Kershaw, *Hitler,* pp. 190–191.

91   "The protest of ordinary people": Kershaw, *Hitler*, p. 196.

92   He pledged to restore prosperity: National WWII Museum, "How Did Hitler Happen?," nationalww2museum.org/war/articles/how-did-hitler-happen.

93   "That historic day was an end and a beginning": Kershaw, *Hitler*, p. 262.

94   TODAY HITLER IS ALL OF GERMANY: Ian Kershaw, "How Hitler Won Over the German People," *Spiegel* Online, Jan. 30, 2008, spiegel.de/international/germany/the-fuehrer-myth-how-hitler-won-over-the-german-people-a-531909.html.

95   Over the next three years: Kater, *Hitler Youth*, pp. 19–23.

96   "It was the most fascinating thing": Quoted in Kater, *Hitler Youth*, p. 68.

97   The Nazi youth movement: U.S. Holocaust Memorial Museum, "Hitler Youth," Oct. 4, 2018, Holocaust Encyclopedia, encyclopedia.ushmm.org/content/en/article/hitler-youth-2.

98   "In 1944, it employed only 32,000": U.S. Holocaust Memorial Museum, "Gestapo," Holocaust Encyclopedia, encyclopedia.ushmm.org/content/en/article/gestapo.

99   He had in mind U.S. immigration laws: James Q. Whitman, "Op-Ed: When the Nazis Wrote the Nuremberg Laws, They Looked to Racist American Statutes," *Los Angeles Times*, Feb. 22, 2017, latimes.com/opinion/op-ed/la-oe-whitman-hitler-american-race-laws-20170222-story.html.

100 "They laid the foundation": U.S. Holocaust Memorial Museum, "Nuremberg Race Laws," encyclopedia.ushmm.org/content/en/article/nuremberg-laws.

101 The rioters destroyed 267 synagogues: U.S. Holocaust Memorial Museum, "Kristallnacht," Holocaust Encyclopedia, encyclopedia.ushmm.org/content/en/article/kristallnacht.

102 "peace with honor": Neville Chamberlain, speech, Sept. 30, 1938, London, in Euro Docs, Howard B. Lee Library, Brigham Young University, eudocs.lib.byu.edu/index.php/Neville_Chamberlain's_%22Peace_For_Our_Time%22_speech.

103 During the war, the Germans murdered: Snyder, *Bloodlands*, pp. x–xi.

104 "dictatorship of evil": Hans Scholl and Alex Schmorell, "Leaflet of the White Rose" [in German], no. 3, June-July 1942, trans. Hermann Feuer, Holocaust Education & Archive Research Team, holocaustresearchproject.org/revolt/wrleaflets.html.

105 "We will not be silent": Hans Scholl, "Leaflet of the White Rose" [in German], no. 4, July 1942, trans. Hermann Feuer, Holocaust Education & Archive Research Team, holocaustresearchproject.org/revolt/wrleaflets.html.

106 "high-stakes 'winner-takes-all' gamble": Kershaw, *Hitler*, p. 871.

107 "An ill-educated beerhall demagogue": Kershaw, *Hitler*, p. 969.

Chapter 5: Man of Steel

108 Young women carrying parasols: The robbery in Tiflis is described more fully in Montefiore, *Young Stalin*, pp. 1–16.

109 "Russia is still struggling": Samuel Rachlin, "Stalin's Long Shadow," *New York Times*, March 4, 2013, nyti.ms/XF1Xk1.

110 They had two children who both died: Montefiore, *Young Stalin*, p. 22.

111 Joseph's father was a harsh: Service, *Stalin*, p. 16.

112 "If there'd been no Lenin": Quoted in A. Mgeladze, *Stalin, kakim ya ego znal. Stranitsy nedavnego prohlogo* (Tbilisi, 2001), p. 82, in Montefiore, *Young Stalin*, p. 75.

113 "Cossacks and bandits": Montefiore, *Young Stalin*, p. 9.

114   "Radical Marxists anticipated civil war": Service, *Stalin*, p. 93.

115   "It was harsher and more desolate": Montefiore, *Young Stalin*, p. 275.

116   "At the height of the crisis": Applebaum, *Red Famine*, p. xxvi.

117   During World War II, a Polish legal scholar: Lemkin, *Axis Rule in Occupied Europe*, p. 79.

118   "means any of the following acts": United Nations Convention on the Prevention and Punishment of the Crime of Genocide, December 9, 1948, hrweb.org/legal/genocide .html.

119   "the physical elimination of an entire ethnic group": Appelbaum, *Red Famine*, p. 417.

120   "Stalin started and maintained the movement": Service, *Stalin*, p. 347.

121   "Joseph Stalin has gone a long way": "Person of the Year: A Photo History," *Time*, content.time.com/time/specials/packages/article/0,28804,2019712_2019694_2019592,00 .html.

122   By early 1939, Soviet prisons: Conquest, *The Great Terror*, pp. 485–486.

123   "The Holocaust overshadows German plans": Snyder, *Bloodlands*, p. x.

124   deaths of some twenty-seven million people: Hastings, *Inferno*, p. 152.

125   "To arrest so many innocent people": Yelchin, *Breaking Stalin's Nose*, Author's Note.

126   "Ideology—that is what gives evildoing": Solzhenitsyn, *The Gulag Archipelago*, pt. 1, p. 173.

127   "The lesson to be learned": Service, *Stalin*, p. 11.

Chapter 6: The Long March

128   Glenn Cowan, an admitted hippie: Griffin, *Ping-Pong Diplomacy*, pp. 188–189.

129   "We simply cannot afford": Richard M. Nixon, "Asia After Viet Nam," *Foreign Affairs* 46, no. 1 (Oct. 1967): p. 121, jstor.org/stable/20039285.

130   "One of them presided over the citadel": Short, *Mao*, p. 610.

131   Mao's father had set up his teenage son: Short, *Mao*, p. 26.

132   Although the marriage was official: Short, *Mao*, pp. 29–30.

133   "I learned that when I defended my rights": Short, *Mao*, p. 26.

134   "The youth of sixteen": Terrill, *Mao*, p. 43.

135   "an empire without wants": Boorstin, *The Discoverers*, p. 195–196.

136   "Thinking the revolution was over": Quoted in Edgar Snow, *Red Star Over China*, rev. ed. (London: Pelican Books, 1972), p. 167, in Short, *Mao*, p. 46.

137   Crossing snowy mountains: Short, *Mao*, p. 329.

138   "When the enemy was not close by": "Long March," History.com, Aug. 21, 2018, history .com/topics/china/long-march.

139   "The Long March is a manifesto": Mao, "On Tactics Against Japanese Imperialism," Dec. 27, 1935, in *Selected Works of Mao Tse-Tung*, vol. 1, p. 160.

140   thousands of young Chinese began: "Long March," History.com.

141   In June 1937, the first picture of Mao: Short, *Mao*, 377–79.

142   "Whatever accords with Mao Zedong Thought": Short, *Mao*, p. 547.

143   two hundred thousand to two million: Roberts, *A Short History of China*, p. 257.

144   hundreds of thousands of businessmen: Roberts, *A Short History of China*, p. 258.

145 "Mao, the Great Helmsman, promised in 1958": Chang, *The Coming Collapse of China*, pp. xxix–xxx.

146 "Mao's appearance was timed to coincide": Short, *Mao*, p. 540.

147 "landlords, rich peasants": Yan Jiaqi and Gao Gao, *Turbulent Decade: A History of the Cultural Revolution*, trans. and ed. D. W. Y. Kwok (Honolulu: University of Hawaii, 1996), p. 76, in Short, *Mao*, p. 542.

148 After Mao's death: Nicholas D. Kristof, "Suicide of Jiang Qing, Mao's Widow, Is Reported," *New York Times*, June 5, 1991, nyti.ms/29nhEZC.

149 there are gruesome accounts: Jing Lin, *The Red Guards' Path to Violence* (New York: Praeger, 1991), p. 23; in Short, *Mao*, p. 542.

150 In a memoir of the period: Li, *Snow Falling in Spring*, p. 60.

151 "He was cold and calculating": Dikötter, *The Cultural Revolution*, p. xiv.

152 A child during the Cultural Revolution: Chen, *China's Son*, pp. 3–6.

153 Mao reportedly liked its resemblance: "Who, What, Why: What Is the Little Red Book?" BBC News Magazine, Nov. 26, 2015, bbc.com/news/magazine-34932800.

154 Among its many tenets, was this "wisdom": *Quotations from Chairman Mao Tsetung* (Peking: Foreign Languages Press, 1972), pp. 3, 11, 13, 61.

155 He was said to have had no use: Short, *Mao*, pp. 19–20.

156 His personal physician: Richard Bernstein, "The Tyrant Mao, as Told by His Doctor," *New York Times*, Oct. 2, 1994, nyti.ms/29jaUfS.

157 the new "Chinese Dream": Bill Bishop, "A Highly Public Trip for China's President, and Its First Lady," DealBook, *New York Times*, March 25, 2013, nyti.ms/32NnAov.

158 "has provided the glue": Short, *Mao*, p. xxix.

Chapter 7: Stalin on the Tigris

159 "It was different from the other bombs": Middle East Watch interview, Halabja, May 17, 1992, in Power, *"A Problem from Hell,"* p. 188.

160 "Halabja quickly became known as the Kurdish Hiroshima": Power, *"A Problem from Hell,"* p. 189.

161 Saddam's mother, Sabha: Jerrold M. Post, "Saddam Hussein," in *Leaders and Their Followers in a Dangerous World: The Psychology of Political Behavior* (Ithaca, NY: Cornell University Press, 2004), p. 211.

162 Saddam Hussein envisioned an Iraqi future: Harvey Sicherman, "Saddam Hussein: Stalin on the Tigris," Foreign Policy Research Institute, Feb. 7, 2007, fpri.org /article/2007/02/saddam-hussein-stalin-tigris/.

163 Saddam assassinated a rival: Makiya, *Republic of Fear*, p. 118.

164 "Hundreds of arrests": MacFarquhar, "Saddam Hussein, Defiant Dictator."

165 "The [Baath Party] developed the politics of fear": Makiya, *Republic of Fear*, p. xi–xii.

166 "The various forms": "Amnesty International Accuses Iraq of Torturing Prisoners," *Washington Post*, April 29, 1981, washingtonpost.com/archive/politics/1981/04/29 /amnesty-international-accuses-iraq-of-torturing-prisoners/2574c72a-bb38-4cbf -b917-eb31d9a5f9fd/.

167 "Guards dragged away each of the accused": Neil MacFarquhar, "Saddam Hussein, Defiant Dictator Who Ruled Iraq with Violence and Fear, Dies," *New York Times*, Dec. 30, 2006, nytimes.com/2006/12/30/world/middleeast/30saddam.html?mtrref=www .google.com&assetType=REGIWALL&auth=login-email.

168 "Saddam Hussein borrowed from Stalinism": Saïd K. Aburish, "Secrets of His Life and Leadership," interview for "The Survival of Saddam," *Frontline*, Jan. 25, 2000, pbs.org /wgbh/pages/frontline/shows/saddam/interviews/aburish.html.

169 "While Mr. Hussein was in power": MacFarquhar, "Saddam Hussein, Defiant Dictator."

170 "Mr. Hussein held on to the ethos": MacFarquhar, "Saddam Hussein, Defiant Dictator."

171 "Victims have described": "Iraq: Systematic Torture of Political Prisoners," Amnesty International, Aug. 2001, amnesty.org/download/Documents/128000/mde140082001en .pdf

172 "For the first five years, he put me in a cell": Quoted in Brian MacQuarrie, "Hussein's Ex-Doctor Hopes to Heal Iraq," *Boston Globe*, Aug. 7, 2003, in "Tales of Saddam's Brutality," Renewal in Iraq, George W. Bush White House, Sept. 29, 2003, georgewbush -whitehouse.archives.gov/news/releases/2003/09/20030929-14.html.

173 "Power is not a means, it is an end": Orwell, *1984*, p. 252.

174 "The dogs were already dead": E. A. Torriero, "Memories Haunt Iraqi 'Cubs,'" *Chicago Tribune*, Aug. 3, 2003, in "Tales of Saddam's Brutality."

175 Under Uday: The details of Uday Hussein's torture of athletes are culled from the clippings collected by the George W. Bush White House in "Tales of Saddam's Brutality."

176 Immanuel Baba Dano, coach of the national soccer team: Robert F. Worth, "Iraqi Athletes Scour Field of Nightmares," *New York Times*, Aug. 17, 2003, nytimes. com/2003/08/17/world/iraqi-athletes-scour-field-of-nightmares.html.

177 Uday also kept two lions caged on a farm: Hala Jaber, Matthew Campbell, and Christina Lamb, "Evil in the Blood," *Sunday Times* (London), July 27, 2003, in "Tales of Saddam's Brutality."

178 "We knew Saddam was tough": Aburish, "Secrets of His Life."

179 "Oil, money, arms, terror": Sicherman, "Saddam Hussein."

180 "Had we gone the invasion route": George Bush and Brent Scowcroft, *A World Transformed* (New York: Vintage, 1999), p. 489.

181 "The rebel fighters": Dave Johns, "The Crimes of Saddam Hussein," PBS, Jan. 24, 2006, pbs.org/frontlineworld/stories/iraq501/events_uprising.html.

182 "The objects unearthed at Iraqi prisons": Erica Goode, "Stalin to Saddam: So Much for the Madman Theory," *New York Times*, May 4, 2003, nytimes.com/2003/05/04 /weekinreview/the-world-stalin-to-saddam-so-much-for-the-madman-theory.html.

183 In Saddam's era, Abu Ghraib: Seymour M. Hersh, "Torture at Abu Ghraib," *New Yorker*, April 30, 2004, newyorker.com/magazine/2004/05/10/torture-at-abu-ghraib.

184 "Army regulations and the Geneva conventions": Hersh, "Torture at Abu Ghraib."

185 "He had an entire room of one palace": Jamie Glazov et al. "Stalin and Saddam: Just What Was the Connection?" reprint from *FrontPage Mag*, April 2003, History News Network, historynewsnetwork.org/article/1382.

186 "The evil that men do lives after them": Shakespeare, *Julius Caesar*, act 3, scene 1.

187 "Like Stalin and Hitler, Mr. Hussein": Goode, "Stalin to Saddam."

188 These type of leaders share four qualities: Elisabeth Bumiller, "Was a Tyrant Prefigured by Baby Saddam?," *New York Times*, May 15, 2004, nytimes.com/2004/05/15 /books/was-a-tyrant-prefigured-by-baby-saddam.html.

189 "who acted out his future": Goode, "The World; Stalin to Saddam," May 4, 2003.

Chapter 8: Never Again?

190   "As I would not be a *slave*": *Collected Works of Abraham Lincoln*, vol. 2, ed. Roy P. Basler (New Brunswick, NJ: Rutgers University Press, 1953), p. 532.

191   "For those denounced by their smug, horrible children": *Selected Works of Stephen Vincent Benét*, vol. 1 (New York: Farrar & Rinehart, 1942).

192   "Mercifully, what happened in Germany in 1933": Ian Kershaw, "How Democracy Produced a Monster," *New York Times*, Feb. 3, 2008, nyti.ms/2jImFjc.

193   "It was knowingly and lightheartedly": Quoted in Power, *"A Problem from Hell,"* p. 23.

194   "Who's going to remember all this riff-raff": Quoted in Jonathan Glover, *Humanity: A Moral History of the Twentieth Century* (New Haven, CT: Yale University Press, 2000), in Power, *"A Problem from Hell,"* p. 522, n16.

195   "one of the major killing grounds of modern times": Hochschild, *King Leopold's Ghost*, p. 3.

196   Idi Amin killed at least three hundred thousand Ugandans: Riccardo Orizio, "Idi Amin's Exile Dream," *New York Times*, Aug. 21, 2003, nytimes.com/2003/08/21/opinion /idi-amin-s-exile-dream.html.

197   thrown to the crocodiles: "Idi Amin, 'Butcher of Uganda,'" CNN, cnn.com/2003 /WORLD/africa/08/16/amin.obituary/index.html; Aug. 16, 2003, and "Idi Amin's island of slaughter for sale," *Daily Telegraph*, June 2, 2002, telegraph.co.uk/news/worldnews /africaandindianocean/uganda/1396120/Idi-Amins-island-of-slaughter-for-sale.html.

198   Stephen Rapp, the U.S. State Department's top war crimes official: Quoted in Josh Rogin, "U.S.: Assad's 'Machinery of Death' Worst Since the Nazis," *Daily Beast*, July 7, 2014, thedailybeast.com/us-assads-machinery-of-death-worst-since-the-nazis.

199   "In Syria and Myanmar, hundreds of thousands": Freedom House, *Freedom in the World 2019: Democracy in Retreat*, Feb. 4, 2019, freedomhouse.org/report/freedom -world/freedom-world-2019/democracy-in-retreat.

200   "these crimes against humanity": United Nations, *Report of the Commission of Inquiry on Human Rights in the Democratic People's Republic of Korea* (New York: United Nations, 2014), summary, pp. 10, 14, ohchr.org/EN/HRBodies/HRC/CoIDPRK/Pages /ReportoftheCommissionofInquiryDPRK.aspx.

201   a net worth of $200 billion by one recent estimate: David Z. Morris, "Vladimir Putin Is Reportedly Richer Than Bill Gates and Jeff Bezos Combined," *Fortune*, July 29, 2017, fortune.com/2017/07/29/vladimir-putin-russia-jeff-bezos-bill-gates-worlds-richest -man/.

202   "The Russians carried out a landmark intervention": Scott Shane and Mark Mazzetti, "The Plot to Subvert an Election: Unraveling the Russia Story So Far," *New York Times*, Sept. 20, 2018, nyti.ms/2NmUclP.

203   In a 2003 poll asking Russians: Gessen, *The Future Is History*, p. 306.

204   "Surely the Board knows what democracy is": E. B. White, "The Meaning of Democracy," *New Yorker*, July 3, 1943, newyorker.com/books/double-take/e-b-white -on-the-meaning-of-democracy.

205   "First they came for the socialists": Quoted in Wolfgang Gerlach, *And the Witnesses Were Silent: The Confessing Church and the Jews*, trans. and ed. Victoria J. Barnett (Lincoln: University of Nebraska Press, 2000), p. 47, in U.S. Holocaust Memorial Museum, "Martin Niemöller: 'First They Came for the Socialists,'" Holocaust Encyclopedia, encyclopedia.ushmm.org/content/en/article/martin-niemoeller-first -they-came-for-the-socialists.

206   "Much controversy surrounds the content": U.S. Holocaust Memorial Museum, "Martin

Niemöller: 'First They Came for the Socialists,'" Holocaust Encyclopedia.

207   "I acted as I had to act": Richard Hansen, *A Noble Treason: The Story of Sophie Scholl and the White Rose Revolt Against Hitler* (San Francisco: Ignatius, 2012), p. 270, in Freedman, *We Will Not Be Silent*, p. 85.

Acknowledgments

208   "The arc of the moral universe": "The Arc of the Moral Universe Is Long, But It Bends Toward Justice," Quote Investigator, quoteinvestigator.com/2012/11/15/arc-of -universe/.

209   "Sites of Conscience": "About Us," International Coalition of Sites of Conscience, www .sitesofconscience.org/en/who-we-are/about-us/.

INDEX